The Fiction of Nathanael West

RANDALL REID

The Fiction of Nathanael West

No Redeemer, No Promised Land

The University of Chicago Press

CHICAGO AND LONDON

ISBN: 0–226–70924–8 (clothbound); 0–226–70925–6 (paperbound)
Library of Congress Catalog Card Number: 67–30949
THE UNIVERSITY OF CHICAGO PRESS, CHICAGO 60637
The University of Chicago Press, Ltd., London

To Jon Chapin
who first introduced me to West's novels
more than a dozen years ago.

Acknowledgments

Though I frequently dissent from his critical judgments, I am heavily indebted to James F. Light for the biographical material collected in his *Nathanael West: An Interpretative Study*. This material, together with the published reminiscences of John Sanford and Josephine Herbst, has obviously allowed me to explore West's reading—and thereby the probable influences on his own work—with more than intuition as a guide. Among West's many commentators, Daniel Aaron deserves special recognition. His various articles on West touch on several points which have been elaborated in later studies, including my own. I am particularly grateful to Thomas Moser for his assistance throughout the preparation of this study, and to Alfred Appel and Albert Guerard for their useful comments.

Permission to quote from the following works has been generously granted by the publishers: *Miss Lonelyhearts* (Copyright 1933 by Nathanael West; 1960 by Laura Perelman), and *The Day of the Locust* (Copyright 1939 by Estate of Nathanael West; 1966 by Laura Perelman), reprinted by permission of New Directions Publishing Corporation; Charles Baudelaire, "An Allegory," from *The Flowers of Evil*, translated by F. P. Sturm and edited by Marthiel and Jackson Mathews (Copyright 1955, 1962, by New Directions), reprinted by permission of New Directions Publishing Corporation; J. K. Huysmans, *Against the*

Grain (New York: Modern Library, 1930), reprinted by permission of Random House, Incorporated; Gilbert Seldes, *The Seven Lively Arts* (New York: Harper & Bros., 1924), and Aldous Huxley, *Antic Hay* (New York: Harper & Bros., 1951), reprinted by permission of Harper and Row, Publishers. References to *The Dream Life of Balso Snell* and *A Cool Million* (Copyright by Estate of Nathanael West) are from *The Complete Works of Nathanael West* (New York: Farrar, Straus and Cudahy, 1957).

Contents

Introduction

I

A critical study of Nathanael West is hardly a novelty. After years of being out of fashion, his work now suffers from another danger, that of being taken for granted. West is routinely cited as a precursor of current literary trends, his name is sure to be dropped in any discussion of the grotesque, and book reviewers automatically compare new Hollywood novels with *The Day of the Locust. Miss Lonelyhearts* has even undergone that ceremony which, in some literary circles, constitutes ritual initiation—two recent critics have detected in it a case of repressed homosexuality.[1] And the number of books and articles devoted to West's work grows so rapidly that a bibliographer has trouble keeping up. There is in all this at least one development which is worthy of simple gratitude—West's books are back in print and available in various paperbacks, foreign editions, and translations. His work is obviously being read, and it deserves to be. But it does not deserve to be fashionable. That West's name should come into vogue at a time when "black humor" is as marketable as sex—and

[1] See Stanley Edgar Hyman, *Nathanael West*, pp. 22–24, and Victor Comerchero, *Nathanael West: The Ironic Prophet*, pp. 84 and 96–100.

often as synthetic as the Playmate of the month—is just a depressing, and peculiarly Westian, joke. It is true that West was in many ways the enemy of his own time, but he was no herald of ours.

West's vogue has not, of course, been complete. None of his books has ever become a campus fad, and none is ever likely to. He frustrates too many of the common motives for reading. West does not invite the reader to see himself as a sensitive soul in a cruel world, a world made cruel by the stupidity and heartlessness of others. Nor does he allow a reader the comforts of superior laughter. In the deflationary world of his books, simple mockery collapses as completely as simple self-pity. So do all the customary poses: ironic detachment, passionate involvement, heartfelt compassion. A reader who wants a simple attitude to take toward his world will therefore get no help from West.

There are other limitations on West's vogue. Though he is now officially recognized even by those scholars and critics who do not like him, he is still classified, often with an almost passionate insistence, as a minor writer. The most obvious reason is that he did not write very much. But many writers—Stephen Crane and F. Scott Fitzgerald, for example—are known for a very small body of work, and if they are not ranked with Tolstoi and Shakespeare, neither are they emphatically denied major status. West is called minor, I suspect, because of what he did write, not because of what he left unwritten. His vision is too narrow, his subjects are too extreme, there are no normal people in his books, and life isn't all like that.[2] Of course it isn't, but the

[2] This theme dominated many of the original reviews of West's novels, and it is still a frequent refrain in informal discussions of his work. It has also been expressed—though not in any way that could be called

same objection could be brought to bear against any work of fiction—or against any view of life whatever. The myth of comprehensive genius is only a myth, even when it is applied to Shakespeare. Yet it is obviously true that some writers are more comprehensive than others, and it is obviously silly to suggest that West's range was Shakespearean. There are good reasons, as well as bad ones, for calling him narrow. But there are also good reasons for calling him complex, wide-ranging, and subtle; and there are even better reasons for saying that, when applied to his work, our usual categories make no sense at all.

Many critics of the thirties ignored West because his books did not conform to the "gravymashpotato"[3] school of social realism. That was only a temporary and particular form of a general complaint: those who believe that the novel must portray with detailed fidelity the surface of life —whether natural or social—must necessarily feel that West fails as a novelist. No one, however, has satisfactorily explained why the novel must attempt such a portrayal, except that most nineteenth-century novels did. The partisans of another and somewhat more recent tradition must also find West unsatisfactory—those who believe that the novel must portray with detailed fidelity the interior of life, whether that portrayal be Jamesian, Joycean, or Proustian. In West's work, the stream of consciousness is almost nonexistent. He disappoints a good many other expectations too. He contrived no ethos of courage (like Hemingway), created no myth of passionate renewal (like Lawrence), por-

---

definitive—in A. M. Tibbets, "The Strange Half-World of Nathanael West." pp. 8–14.

[3] I have borrowed the phrase from Angel Flores' review of *Miss Lonely-hearts*. See "Miss Lonelyhearts in the Haunted Castle," p. 1.

trayed no great external dramas (like Tolstoi), refurbished
no traditional beliefs (like Eliot), advanced no dogmas, bol-
stered no hopes, soothed no fears. It is therefore fair to ask
what he did do, for he begins to sound narrow indeed.
Perhaps, as is so often remarked, he anticipated literary
trends which have flourished since. Perhaps, but West's
influence on contemporary writing still seems to me hard to
evaluate. A few writers—notably John Hawkes and Flan-
nery O'Connor—have acknowledged him as a literary ancestor, but neither his tone nor the peculiar logic which
controlled his use of the grotesque is widely reflected in
current fiction. And I see no reason why they should be.
Much of West's interest lies in his odd relationship to all
literary fashions, even those which have succeeded him. He
resists assimilation. And the easy vagueness of our literary
definitions betrays us totally when we apply them to West.
Except in its worst and most imitative forms, the grotesque
is not a single mode.[4] William Burroughs and Thomas Pyn-
chon, for example, have only a limited connection with
each other, let alone with West, and we achieve nothing
but confusion by classifying them together. We achieve
even less by making West the precursor of something so
inclusive as "anti-realism." He was often an extremely realistic writer. Though his name is invoked to sanction the
distortion of reality, though distortion is obviously present

---

[4] There are, of course, certain ways in which all grotesques can be said
to resemble each other—they are all "distorted," and usually they are
distorted from the human to the mechanical, the animal, or the stereo-
typical. West's grotesques, like those of more recent writers, bear these
generic attributes, but the resemblance is so generic that its significance
seems to me slight. The influences of grotesque art in general and of
Faulkner in particular are probably more responsible for contemporary
trends than West is.

in his novels, he frequently dropped it in favor of a scrupulous attention to the external scene which Flaubert would have admired. The cock fight in *The Day of the Locust* is, for example, as fine a bit of realistic description as anyone could want. And West is the permanent enemy of all "non-realistic" visions fed on mushrooms or LSD. In his work, most hallucination is involuntary and dreadful, not euphoric. The "oceanic feeling" is simply a late stage of hysteria. And the expansive vision of any kind—whether comic, horrible, or ecstatic—has no place in his books. West's use of hallucination is radically lucid and controlled, not "wild."

It is not, therefore, much easier to find West a niche which will hold him now than it was when he was alive. He is a curious figure. Though his work was obviously "original," he is almost as hard to parody as he is to imitate. Most grotesque characters—Steinbeck's Lennie and O'Neill's Hairy Ape are obvious examples—are so easy to ridicule that they are exploited by popular comedians. West's characters, despite their grotesqueness, somehow evade the parodist's grasp. Even his style is elusive. Unlike the various syles of Hemingway, Faulkner, and the later James, it does not invite easy burlesque. Why? Perhaps for the same reason that West resists easy classification by literary critics. Parody, like caricature, usually hunts for the distinctive feature which can be exaggerated, but it is hard to extract the distinctive feature from West's work. He was always the writer of mixed vision, mixed attitudes, mixed modes. And parody, again like caricature, also hunts for the pretentious feature, but West's style is least pretentious when it is most distinctive. At its best, it is a style so simple that it does not even strive for the effect of simplicity. There is a final reason, of course: West was a parodist himself, as completely a parodist as anyone who ever wrote "serious" novels.

This last remark should startle no one—except, perhaps, those who may wonder why anyone should want to proclaim the self-evident. But the self-evident is often confusing precisely because it is obvious. We all know what parody is, and we are nearly all sure that it should not be taken very seriously. Like detective stories and light verse, parodies are usually funneled out of the mainstream of literature into separate anthologies where they can be happy in the company of their peers. There are exceptions, of course. When parody appears in a book like *Ulysses*, it cannot just be exiled to the humorous anthologies. Often it creates the same sort of embarrassment that smut does, and we are likely to hunt around for redeeming social or literary values to justify its presence. We do not, however, gain much by trading condescension for ponderous solemnity. And one problem in discussing parody is that we have grown used to taking certain forms of it very seriously indeed. The combination of parody, pastiche, allusion, and direct quotation in the work of Joyce and Eliot is so familiar and so admired that it constitutes a modern orthodoxy.[5] Orthodoxies are always dangerous, especially to the heretic. West was not just a follower of Joyce or Eliot, and if we apply the usual terms to his use of parody we are almost sure to miss the point. Yet the terms are not irrelevant. West was, to con-

---

[5] The literary methods of Joyce and Eliot are hardly identical, of course. The separate influence of each has, however, combined to produce some common assumptions about the use of traditional materials, ironic parallels, and verbal puns or allusions. Orthodox critical assumptions are likely to distort our understanding of anything, even of those writers from whom they are derived.

tinue the religious analogy, a heretic, not a pagan. He knew
the modern orthodoxies, observed their rituals and borrowed their texts, but insisted on reading them by his own
light. His parodies are interesting for this reason alone: they
provide a commentary on most of the literary fashions of
our century, including some which are still current.

The uses of parody are not, however, limited to ridicule
or even to irony. The parodist is a mimic. His fundamental
skill is the ability to imitate the familiar, and his performance may arouse that "pure" delight which any triumphant
virtuosity does. It may also reveal unfamiliar qualities hidden in familiar styles. Parody can be a form of experimental
writing, a way of testing the further possibilities of a familiar form. When a parodist has mastered the art of simple
mimicry, it is natural for him to begin to play with his
impersonations. What happens to a style when it is twisted
slightly, or combined with another style, or detached from
its usual subjects and applied to new ones? West was fond
of these experiments; indeed, much of his originality lies,
paradoxically, in the use he made of borrowed materials.

At this point, the discussion of parody as a distinct form
seems about to disappear into the normal question of literary sources and influences. In some ways it inevitably
does—it is always hard to keep one's categories straight
when talking about West. But there is an important distinction to be preserved. Unlike other writers, a parodist is
necessarily very conscious of his sources. When he imitates
something, he knows what he is doing. He does not simply
absorb the influence of certain literary masters or traditions
from the atmosphere about him. If he is a good parodist, he
must be conscious not only of what he is imitating at the
moment but of what he isn't; he must know the distinctive

accents that separate one style from another. This necessary consciousness can easily pass into self-consciousness. If a parodist is inescapably aware of every echo in his voice, he may find it difficult to speak—difficult, at least, to speak in any tones except those of deliberate parody. But he may also find it necessary to speak. How? He is extraordinarily sensitive to banality, but his vocabulary is restricted to clichés—indeed, to him the resources of the language may seem restricted to clichés. The alternatives are mockery and fatuity. Obviously, these alternatives are inadequate. But to the parodist they may seem inescapable—unless, that is, he can make banality eloquent or turn mockery against itself. Or unless he can find a substitute for language. West attempted each of these methods—even, in a curious sense, the last of them.

I am, of course, aware of an immediate objection. To say that West used a substitute for language is, in every normal sense, obviously absurd—his pages contain nothing but words, nearly all of which can be found in any standard dictionary—but it is an absurdity which I shall retain. We naturally borrow the vocabulary of other arts and other experiences whenever we talk about literature: we speak of the "architecture" of novels, of the "orchestration" of dialogue, of the "painting" of scenes, even of the "fragrance" of a style. Such talk is dangerous—it is always threatened by the risks inherent in metaphors on the one hand and clichés on the other—but it is sometimes useful. In talking about West, it is very nearly inescapable. When he remarked that he originally conceived of *Miss Lonelyhearts* as a novel in the form of a cartoon strip, he was not, of course, simply being cute. The conception was serious, and much of it shows in the final version of *Miss Lonelyhearts.*

His images, like those in cartoons, have a way of detaching themselves from the text. Even though they are conveyed through words, they form in the reader's consciousness a distinct set of pictures—pictures which are somehow different from those which a novelist usually evokes by describing a scene. The reason is simple. West was a pictorial parodist quite as much as he was a literary one. He "drew" his characters and scenes in recognizable styles borrowed from nearly all the graphic media. The odd juxtaposition of these styles with each other and with the speech of West's characters creates much of the peculiar tension of his novels. It also distinguishes him from such "painterly" writers as Hawthorne and James who, in their different ways, worked in fairly constant styles. West's style was never constant. At times his pictorial technique closely resembles collage—but only at times. It also resembles cartoon strips, movies, and several different schools of painting, as well as such non-graphic visual arts as the tableau and the dance.

It should begin to be apparent that West was, in several ways, a "formal" writer. He deliberately employed an intricate set of conventions, and if we do not understand these conventions we are not likely to understand his novels. We have often been told, by Aristotle and others, that art is imitation. We usually assume that it is in some sense an imitation of life. But in what sense? In West's novels, the immediate object of imitation is often neither "reality" nor "fantasy" as we commonly define those terms. Instead, it is some form of "art." The distinction is fundamental but by no means simple. To begin with, it separates West from both "realism" and "anti-realism," though he has some characteristics of both schools. It also complicates our use of words like "distortion." We can say, whether or not we

should, that Picasso's *Three Musicians* distorts reality, and
at least be fairly sure of what we mean. But what do we
mean when we say that someone parodying Picasso has
distorted reality? Do we mean that his picture distorts nature as we commonly perceive it or that it distorts Picasso's
style as we commonly perceive it? We could, of course,
mean either of these things—or both of them—but we
should be careful to make our meaning clear. As objects,
Picasso's paintings are part of external reality, and to imitate
them is to imitate reality. The observation is trite but fairly
important. Another observation is even more trite and more
important: life imitates art. The power of art to shape
reality—the reality we enact as well as the reality we perceive—is a persistent theme in West's novels. It is also a
persistent motive for his multiple use of parody. Whether
or not Picasso's paintings resemble life, life will, in time,
begin to resemble Picasso's paintings.

For a "narrow" writer, West begins to seem rather complicated. There is, of course, no necessary contradiction
between "narrow" and "complicated," and there is no point
in applying either term until we have examined West's
novels more closely. I think West is worth the examination.
In a century which has made experimental writing almost
an absolute value, he is one of the more interesting innova-
tors. The words we like to use to describe modern literature—"violence," "the grotesque," "decadence," "dream,"
"irony," "allusion," "distortion," "realism," "tradition,"
"experiment"—are all applicable to his work. So are
a good many other words, both in and out of fashion.
Though West anticipated new literary trends, he also incorporated many trends which had already flourished, some
of them for centuries.

There are other reasons for examining West's novels. Though he was a formal writer who made deliberate use of conventions, it is also true that he dealt explicitly and pointedly with themes. No one was ever less the disinterested aesthete. And perhaps no one has understood so well, or revealed so accurately, the nature of our favorite lies. We have not lost our taste for lying and we have not improved on West's analysis. Neither those who denounce television nor those who have made Batman a Camp hero can tell us as much about popular culture as West does. Here, as always, he is the enemy of simple enthusiasms—of both the denouncers and the applauders, the hip and the square, the hot and the cool. He regarded popular culture with ruthless sympathy; he understood it too well to like it and too well to feel superior to it. If there is "nothing to root for"[6] in such an attitude, there is something to learn from.

Ruthless sympathy is seldom comforting. Dreams were West's special subject, but absolute clarity was his special tool, and clarity is not kind to dreams. Perhaps it is the *absence* of distortion which really shocks. West chose to reveal his "peculiar half-world"[7] without the softening effect of half-light. His subjects are acutely focused, his style is lucid and exact, and his plots culminate in a violence whose logic is unpleasantly plain. The ease with which West made familiar premises yield disastrous conclusions is

---

[6] The phrase is West's own. It occurs in a letter to George Milburn, and it has been widely quoted as an explanation of the failure of West's work to appeal to the radical press, the highbrow press, and the public at large. "There is," said West, "nothing to root for in my work and what is even worse, no rooters." See Richard Gehman's Introduction to *The Day of the Locust*, p. xxii.

[7] Again, the phrase is West's. It is from a letter to Jack Conroy quoted in Gehman's Introduction to *The Day of the Locust*, and it defines the world West tried to create in that novel.

disturbing in itself—far more disturbing than the usual cries
of personal anguish or cosmic despair. And it is quite different from them. Apocalypse is, in West, not an assertion but
the natural consequence of a process. Irreconcilable truths
breed disruptive forces. In his mixed vision it is simultaneously true, for example, that dreams are destructive and
false and that dreams are inescapable. He denies our fantasies but leaves us prisoners of them. The implications of this
paradox, whether or not they are final, are as serious as they
are unpleasant. Our debt to West is that he revealed them
so clearly, revealed them in ways no one else has. He is still
a curious figure. He repudiated social realism but focused
on sociological themes, dismissed psychological novels but
was an acute literary psychologist, laughed at art but was a
conscious and dedicated artist. He was a dandy with proletarian sympathies, a comic writer who specialized in unfunny jokes.

The Dream Life
of Balso Snell:
THROUGH THE PORTALS OF ART

By critical consensus, *The Dream Life of Balso Snell* is a
juvenile and obscure attack on all art, an incoherent parody
which is interesting chiefly because it foreshadows some of
the themes which preoccupied West in *Miss Lonelyhearts*.
It has been called "scatological and pretentiously wise,"[1] "a
sneer in the bathroom mirror at Art,"[2] "schoolboyish,"[3]
"immature . . . [but] the key to all his later works,"[4] and
"a hysterical, obscure, disgusted shriek against the intellect."[5] None of these remarks is definitive, but only the last
one is, I think, flatly wrong. One can certainly find in *Balso
Snell* much that is scatological, schoolboyish, and anticipa-

[1] Daniel Aaron, "The Truly Monstrous: A Note on Nathanael West,"
p. 100.

[2] Alan Ross, "The Dead Center: An Introduction to Nathanael West,"
The Complete Works of Nathanael West, p. xii.

[3] Hyman, p. 15.

[4] Comerchero, p. 51.

[5] James F. Light, *Nathanael West: An Interpretative Study*, p. 59. Light
also asserts that "West accepts the idea, if not the prose, of Joyce's 'yes'
to the body," (p. 56), and he reads the conclusion of *Balso* as a "glorifi-
cation of the physical man" (p. 59), even taking as serious statement the
outrageous parody of mystical union which accompanies Balso's orgasm
(p. 60).

tory of West's later work, but it is not hysterical, its tone is not that of a shriek, and its obscurity is, particularly in a century which has enshrined *Ulysses* and *The Waste Land*, comparatively slight. Despite its multiple allusions, it can be understood without much trouble. The fundamental problem in *Balso Snell* involves incoherence of a different kind. The problem can be stated in several ways, the simplest of which is that much of *Balso* is very funny but some of it isn't. It jumps from jokes which are leaden and obvious to parodies which are the virtuoso performances of a sophisticated stylist. The seduction speeches and responses between Balso and Miss McGeeney are, I think, as compact, skillful, and hilarious as any parodies we have. But the moments when Balso is calling his guide "Stinker" are as bad as anything in any college humor magazine. Such unevenness may be more inevitable than odd. *Balso Snell* was obviously an exploratory book, one in which West tested not only his own talents but the possibilities inherent in the materials he was borrowing. For that reason alone it deserves a closer look than it usually gets.

Scatology as a Comic Conceit

Balso Snell, like *Gulliver's Travels*, begins with an ingenious device. Balso finds the Trojan horse, enters it through the anus, and goes on a picaresque journey through its bowels, encountering a variety of would-be writers and camp followers of the arts during his journey. The gimmick is, however, at least partly borrowed and parodied, not invented. According to S. J. Perelman, West was the first man on the Brown campus to read *Jurgen*,[6] and both the

---

[6] Cited by Hyman, p. 6.

character of Balso and the initial conception of his plot seem to owe more to Cabell than to any other source. Both Jurgen and Balso are middle-aged bourgeois poets; both begin their fantastic journeys by entering a dark cave; both yearn for their lost youth and the lost loves of their youth; both embrace youthful maidens who suddenly turn middle-aged in their arms; both encounter figures representative of the mythic and religious heritage of Western culture; both meet the incarnations of their lost loves; both find that all things end in sex and that sex ends in disenchantment; both even show a comic tendency to make speeches before abandoning themselves to the amorous event. The parody is, of course, generic as well as specific. In many ways Cabell is simply one specimen of a school whose primary characteristics can be found in several other writers, notably Anatole France—the school of affected paganism-genteel eroticism-playful irony-sentimental regret-Olympian resignation. Appropriately, Balso dismisses Christian mysticism as "morbid," finds Gilson's sexual revelations disgusting but is himself perpetually on the make, and repeatedly apostrophizes the past, especially his own— " 'Ah youth!' he sighed elaborately. 'Ah Balso Snell!' "[7]

The plot of *Jurgen* focuses upon a journey into the past. In West's parody, the journey takes place within a concrete relic of the past (the Trojan horse), and *Jurgen's* dark cave is transformed into the anus of that relic. The parody is, from the first, even more ludicrously and intricately "scatological" than is usually recognized. The "anus" here is not

[7] *The Dream Life of Balso Snell* in *The Complete Works of Nathanael West*, p. 23. Subsequent references are to the same edition and are indicated by page numbers in parentheses.

just an anus—it is a horse's ass. The name "Balso Snell" is itself, I think, a thinly disguised variant of "asshole smell"—with perhaps an overtone of "Branch Cabell"—and Balso's initials are a familiar abbreviation.[8] The "scatological" detail hardly ends here, of course. It is immediately followed with "O Anus Mirabilis!" (p. 3), with Balso's "round as the Anus" song (p. 4), with the Phoenix Excrementi, with the fable about the snake who lived in the colon of Appolonius [*sic*] of Tyana, with Doughty's "cloaca" epigram about the Jews, with George Moore and the theory of art as "a sublime excrement" (p. 8), with Gilson's "diarrhoea of words" (p. 14) and his "constipation of desire" (p. 27), with Samuel Perkins and his "excrement period" (p. 34), and with so many other excremental images or metaphors that it is impossible to list them.

The scatology is obviously there, but what is it doing there? We can, of course, simply repeat the usual remarks about the juvenile desire to shock or about the juvenile delight in toilet humor, or about West's "anguished" loathing of the flesh. We can, but I do not think we should. These remarks may be relevant, but their relevance can be demonstrated only after we have noticed more obvious reasons for the "scatology." To begin with, it is a joke—an ingenious and complicated joke. The joke is also highly

---

[8] James F. Light glosses the name as "balls of Snell" (p. 51), but such a gloss is both unrelated to the novel's prevailing joke and undermined by a fact which Light himself cites: "The surname of a Brown professor, who also coached baseball, was Snell, and that name greatly amused West because of its closeness to 'smell'" (p. 30). Victor Comerchero has mentioned the obvious meaning of the initials (n. 18, pp. 177–78). West was obviously fond of obscene puns. We need only recall the Miss Farkis of *Miss Lonelyhearts*, whose name is a resonant chord of simultaneous obscenities, and the sodomitic Prince Kanurani of *A Cool Million*.

indelicate, and I shall compound the indelicacy by explaining it.

Comic writers have always delighted in taking metaphors literally, especially metaphors which are trite or pretentious. We need only recall the kind of fun Swift had with words like "inspiration," or the scene in *The Frogs* where scales are brought out to "weigh" the poetry of Aeschylus and Euripides. It is the classic device of ridicule through comic reduction. With his scatological use of the Trojan horse, West here manages the simultaneous reduction of several themes:

> *First, the journey into the past.*—Balso reverses the normal direction of time by reversing the normal direction of the digestive process; he journeys *up* the alimentary canal. The "Qualis . . . Artifex . . . Pereo" inscribed on the anus is, in view of what an anus actually sees pass away, a ludicrous commentary on nostalgia. The longing for the past is ridiculed totally. It is not even a desire to return to the womb, but a desire to return to the bowels. Organic concepts of time—whether Bergsonian or simply those clichés in which the future is "born from the womb of the past"—are ridiculed by the same device. In West's parody, organic time is digestive, not gestative. It produces no new births, only a fecal residue.
>
> *Second, the pretentiousness of the artist.*—George Moore's statement that art is not nature but nature digested yields the conclusion that art is a sublime excrement—which in turn yields the comically literal vision of artists dwelling in the intestines of the Trojan horse and producing the B. S. suggested by Balso's initials. The Trojan horse itself adds several twists to the joke. It is, of course, a classic symbol of deceit. It is also an imitation horse, not a living one, and the phoniness of the world of art is thereby underscored—even the excrement is unreal.

Third, the decadence of modern life and art.—The Trojan horse is a relic of the ancient world, and the collection
of modern intellectuals and writers who live just inside its
anus are, to put it as euphemistically as possible, derivative.
Like the " 'tin can[s] on the tail of Dr. Johnson' " (p. 33),
they tediously attempt to exploit a vanished greatness.
They quote, they allude, they pose—and their profundi-
ties and their poses have been so thoroughly digested in
past ages that only excrement remains. In terms of West's
comic reduction, the derivative becomes the fecal. There
is a further parody—that of the fashionable stance of
decadence and of ironic contrasts between a vulgar present and a glamorous past. West later offered his own
serious version of this theme, but it had important differences from the fashion he parodied here. And the fashion
was endemic. Eliot's *Prufrock* and *Waste Land*, Flaubert's
lush evocations of the past in contrast to his merciless
revelation of the present, the symbolists, the *fin de siècle*
decadents, Machen and France and Cabell—all sounded a
note of contempt for modern vulgarity and of longing for
the past. In the character of Samuel Perkins, Smeller, West
unites several themes which he took from the symbolists in
general and from that arch-decadent Huysmans in particular: the synthesis of all sense experience into the sensations of a single faculty (smell), the separation of art from
life (Perkins marries "as an artist," not as a man), interest
in the perverse, and the importance of odors as evocations
of the past (Baudelaire and Proust, as well as Huysmans,
of course). Here, the artist as smeller furnishes another
variation on the obscene pun of Balso's name. The decadent aesthete becomes, in the reductive parody, a sniffer of
the asshole smell of the past.

Fourth, the parody of monism.—Balso's "Round as the
anus" song is followed by the guide's discussion of monism
versus pluralism in which a circle is offered as the perfect
monistic symbol: " 'Moreover, if everything is one . . .
then everything is a circle' " (p. 9). The Anus Mirabilis is

here the emblem and the agent of a comic monism. The apparently different substances ingested by the horse ultimately issue from the Anus Mirabilis as a single substance, a familiar and most unmetaphysical substance.

The variations on this joke do not end even here. We need not explore them further, however, for it should be clear that the "scatology" is not simply willful, but an embodiment of the basic parody itself. And the scatological joke employs an appropriately fatuous protagonist. "Middle-aged" and "bourgeois" are probably the key terms to describe Balso. His speech is almost wholly composed of two kinds of cliché: the Philistine and the Romantic. To his Jewish guide, he says: " 'Some of my best friends are Jews' " (p. 8). To Maloney the Areopagite, he says: " 'I think you're morbid. . . . Play games. Don't read so many books. Take cold showers. Eat more meat.' " (p. 13.) Of Gilson's crime journal, he says: " 'Interesting psychologically, but is it art?' " And he offers Gilson his usual advice: " 'Read less and play baseball' " (p. 23). These philistinisms are matched by his equally bourgeois insistence upon romanticizing sex, the past, the role of the artist, and himself. Though Jurgen seems to have provided the initial inspiration, West loads Balso with a variety of characteristics taken from a variety of sources. Balso's " 'O Beer! O Meyerbeer! O Bach! O Offenbach! Stand me now as ever in good stead' " obviously parodies Joyce's invocation in *Portrait of the Artist*.[9] His seduction speeches, with their pastiche of *carpe diem* poetry and the "rational" philosophy of Bertrand Russell, touch a good many targets—aging Bohemians and the disciples of Russell and Isadora Duncan

[9] This obvious point has been frequently noted. See Light, pp. 55-56, and Comerchero, p. 54.

among them. And the parody of philistinism is general indeed; its target could be glossed as "parents, teachers, and other squares."

Protean Clichés

Immediately after entering the Anus Mirabilis, Balso encounters spokesmen for the two major traditions of Western culture: the classical and the Christian. The first encounter rambles through some miscellaneous buffoonery, and ends with the spokesman involved in a subtle, erudite, and apparently endless philosophical discussion, chiefly with himself. The second ends with the spokesman sobbing hysterically over the martyrdom of St. Puce, a flea who lived in the arm pit of Our Lord. In each case, the parody is obvious enough. The burlesque of Christian mysticism, however, involves a few details which may need comment. Maloney the Areopagite is, when Balso encounters him, "naked except for a derby in which thorns were sticking" and "attempting to crucify himself with thumbtacks" (pp. 9–10). The derby has been called a "surrealistic . . . incongruity,"[10] but I suspect it is also a comic congruity. In the symbolism of dreams, said Freud, "hat" equals "phallus," and the devout Maloney attempts to mortify the flesh by wearing thorns in his derby. West thereby doubles his joke. The thumbtacks and the derby travesty the original nails and crown of thorns, but the derby, with its Freudian implications, also travesties the ascetic impulse and perhaps Freudian symbols as well.[11] St. Puce is an even more

---

[10] Comerchero, p. 56.

[11] Max Ernst, one of West's favorite painters, once executed a similar Freudian joke—a painting of hats piled up into phallic shapes which is entitled "The Hat Makes the Man."

elaborate joke. The comic possibilities in Benedict Labre's veneration of those "jewels of sanctity," the vermin infesting his clothes, are multiple, and West misses none of them. Canonizing a flea merely exaggerates Labre's attitude, an attitude which is already bizarre enough to the unbeliever. And the other travesties—of the Eucharist, the Immaculate Conception, martyrdom, fetishistic worship of relics, mystical ecstasy over the flesh of Christ—are all natural extensions of the basic joke. Like the Trojan horse, St. Puce is almost too fertile in comic possibilities.

West is supposed to have been widely read in the Lives of the Saints, but the details he cites here prove only, as so many other things in his work do, that he read Huysmans with some attention. All of the mystics he mentions—Saint Hildegarde, Marie Alacoque, Suso, Labre, Lydwine of Schiedam, Rose of Lima—are discussed in Huysmans' *Là Bas* and *En Route*, and Maloney's citation of "that terrible statement of Saint Hildegarde's, 'The Lord dwells not in the bodies of the healthy and vigorous' " is, with the omission of a parenthetical phrase, an exact quotation from *En Route*.[12] The parody is, I suggest, directed at Huysmans in particular as much as it is at Catholic mysticism in general. After his return to the Church, Huysmans focused his "decadent" instincts upon asceticism as relentlessly as he had earlier focused them upon aesthetic and sexual novelties.

[12] See Joris-Karl Huysmans, *En Route*, p. 222. In Paul's translation, the line is rendered: "that terrible phrase of Saint Hildegarde, a phrase at once just and sinister: 'The Lord dwells not in the bodies of the healthy and vigorous.' " For Huysmans' discussion of the Catholic mystics, see pp. 38–40, 69, 98–99, 134–35, and 292–94 of *En Route;* also *Là Bas*, trans. Keene Wallis, p. 189. West refers to Huysmans in both *Balso Snell* and *Miss Lonelyhearts*, and he is known to have read Huysmans extensively while at Brown. See Light, pp. 24 and 28.

Maloney's thorns and thumbtacks recall, at least in a general way, Huysmans' description of Suso.

> Would you like to imitate Suso, who, to subdue his passions, bore on his naked shoulders, for eighteen years, an enormous cross set with nails, whose points pierced his flesh? More than that, he imprisoned his hands in leather gloves which also bristled with nails, lest he should be tempted to dress his wounds.[13]

And the life of St. Puce, with its "ecstatic" evocation of the perfumes of Christ's flesh, also seems to owe more than a little to Huysmans' style. Huysmans is, at least to an unsympathetic reader, often unintentionally hilarious.

> When Saint Francis de Paul and Venturini of Bergamo offered the Sacrifice they smelt sweet. Saint Joseph of Cupertino secreted such fragrant odours that his track could be followed. . . .
> The pus of Saint John of the Cross and the Blessed Didée gave forth strong and distinct scent of lilies; Barthole, the tertiary, gnawed to the bones by leprosy, gave out pleasant emanations, and the same was the case with Lidwine, Ida of Louvain, Saint Colette, Saint Humiliana, Maria-Victoria of Genoa, Dominic of Paradise, whose wounds were boxes of perfume, whence fresh scents escaped.
> And thus we can enumerate organs and senses one after another, and declare marvellous effects. Without speaking of those faithful stigmata which open or shut according to the Proper of the liturgical year. . . .[14]

Even Maloney's imitation of Notker Balbus [sic], Ekkenard [*sic*] le Vieux, and Hucbald le Chauve (p. 10) echoes Huysmans' own fondness for the poetry and music of the

[13] *En Route*, p. 99.
[14] *Ibid.*, pp. 222–23.

medieval Church, a fondness West alluded to in *Miss Lonelyhearts*.[15]

Balso's encounter with John Gilson, the schoolboy in short pants who writes "Russian" journals so he can sleep with his teacher, introduces a parody figure nearly as generic as Balso. Gilson's precocity—literary and sexual—is a joke in itself. It obviously recalls both the *enfants terribles* who appeared in the pages of Cocteau and Gide and those precocious apostles of the "modern" whom the surrealists adopted as saints: Rimbaud, whose poetic career was over at nineteen; Lautréamont, who died at twenty-four; Jarry, who wrote *Ubu Roi* when he was fifteen.[16] Just as Balso parodies the middle-aged and bourgeois, Gilson parodies the precocious and avant-garde. And the parody is probably self-parody as well. West, we should remember, had read Dostoevski, Tolstoi, and Flaubert by the time he was thirteen, and the first draft of *Balso Snell* was written while he was still in college.[17] Gilson's short pants are surely, among other things, West's way of ridiculing himself.

Though it is surrounded by farce, Gilson's Journal introduces a sudden shift in tone. It is a skillful pastiche, not a broad parody. The description of the murder deliberately evokes echoes of *Crime and Punishment*, Gide's *acte gratuit*, and Freudian analyses of motive, but the imitation is not ridiculous.[18] The narrator is himself quite aware of his imitations.

[15] The newspapermen in the speakeasy refer to Miss Lonelyhearts' approach to God as "too damn literary—plain song, Latin poetry, medieval painting, Huysmans, stained-glass windows and crap like that." West, *Complete Works*, p. 83.

[16] I am indebted here to Wallace Fowlie's *Age of Surrealism*, p. 104.

[17] Light, pp. 8 and 31.

[18] The echoes of Gide and Dostoevski here have been noted by both Light, p. 45, and Hyman, p. 14.

> Sometimes my name is Raskolnikov, sometimes it is
> Iago. I never was, and never shall be, plain John
> Gilson—honest, honest Iago, yes, but never honest John.
> (P. 14.)
>
> When a baby, I affected all the customary poses: I
> "laughed the icy laughter of the soul," I uttered "universal
> sighs"; I sang in "silver-fire verse"; I smiled the "enigmatic
> smile"; I sought "azure and elliptical routes". . . . Along
> with "mon hysterie" I cultivated a "rotten, ripe maturity."
> You understand what I mean: like Rimbaud, I practiced
> having hallucinations. (P. 16.)

There are moments in Gilson's journal when the note of
ridicule clearly does sound—"Reality! Reality! If I could
only discover the Real" (p. 14)—but there are other moments when it disappears entirely.

> Have you ever spent any time among the people who
> farm the great libraries: the people who search old issues
> of the medical journals for pornography and facts about
> strange diseases; the comic writers who exhume jokes
> from old magazines; the men and women employed by the
> insurance companies to gather statistics on death? I
> worked in the philosophy department. That department is
> patronized by alchemists, astrologers, cabalists, demonolo-
> gists, magicians, atheists, and the founders of new religious
> systems. (P. 17.)

And there are still other moments when West seems to try
his hand at a little "serious" writing with parody as a
protective cover. His prose, even if it is imitative, is sometimes cleaner and more compact than the originals.

> On my way back to Broadway I passed some sailors,
> and felt an overwhelming desire to flirt with them. I went
> through all the postures of a desperate prostitute; I
> camped for all I was worth. The sailors looked at me and
> laughed. I wanted very much for one of them to follow

me. Suddenly I heard the sound of footsteps behind me. The steps came close and I felt as though I were melting—all silk and perfumed, pink lace. I died the little death. But the man went past without noticing me. I sat down on a bench and was violently sick. (P. 22.)

If this is parody, its tone is very distant from the broad farce of " 'O Bach! O Offenbach! Stand me now as ever in good stead' " (p. 4). Farce immediately returns, however, when Balso puts down the journal and regards the youthful Gilson himself. Gilson dismisses his journals as "ridiculous," says he wrote them only to seduce Miss McGeeney, and recites a love poem which is as ludicrously bad as Balso's song. Gilson concludes:

"I'm fed up with poetry and art. Yet what can I do. I need women and because I can't buy them or force them, I have to make poems for them. God knows how tired I am of using the insanity of Van Gogh and the adventures of Gauguin as can-openers for the ambitious Count Six-Times." (P. 23.)

The first thing to say about this speech is that it is hardly the "message" of the novel.[19] Gilson has not abandoned poses and confessed his real motive; rather, he has simply substituted one pose for another. His new pose is again neatly antithetical to Balso's—Balso is the Romanticizer; Gilson is the Debunker. The brash cynicism Gilson affects is, of course, a familiar form of precocity. It was also a fashionable stance in the twenties, one which West neatly dissected in *Miss Lonelyhearts*.[20] More broadly, it is simply

---

[19] James Light, however, seems to read this passage as West's own opinion. See Light, pp. 45–46.

[20] The newspapermen in the speakeasy tell their "childish" and endless stories of three-name lady writers who all need a "good rape."

one form of that pose of affected disdain which is as familiar as its antithesis—the pose of passionate personal involvement.

Gilson's Pamphlet, according to Gilson, outlines his "real" position. Actually, it largely elaborates the materials of the Journal: self-conscious awareness of one's literary poses, profound irritation which can neither be relieved nor expressed, an imagination which strains for the novel, a violent act, a résumé of possible motives which fails to explain. Despite the description of the "chaffeur within," the narrator's motives are hardly reducible to "The Desire to Procreate." The sources of his discomfort are multiple and ultimately obscure, and his irritation with Saniette is only partly related to the necessity of wooing her with extravagant poses. His irritation is also the "natural antipathy pessimists feel for optimists" (p. 25). The narrator despises Saniette because she refuses to acknowledge pain, especially his pain. He indulges his revenge by picturing Saniette's death.

> Hiding under the blankets of her hospital bed and invoking the aid of Mother Eddy and Doctor Coué: "I won't die! I am getting better and better. I won't die! The will is master o'er the flesh. I won't die!" Only to have Death answer: "Oh, yes you will." And she had. I made Death's triumph my own. (P. 25.)

Even the narrator's acting hardly bears out Gilson's assertion that art is just a technique for seduction. Though his "relations with Saniette were exactly those of performer and audience," it is not just the necessity of performing but the stupidity and triviality of his audience that annoys him.

> While living with me, Saniette accepted my most desperate feats in somewhat the manner one watches the

marvelous stunts of acrobats. Her casualness excited me so
that I became more and more desperate in my performances. (Pp. 25–26.)

The narrator's attempt to explain his beating of Saniette is
ignored by both Saniette and the clerk. When he mentions
the Marquis de Sade and Gilles de Rais, however, "the clerk
bowed and left us with a smile. Saniette was also of the
world; she smiled and went back to bed" (p. 29). The
narrator makes a second attempt at explanation: "Because
of the phrasing of my complaint, Saniette was able to turn
my revenge into a joke. She weathered a second beating
with a slow, kind smile" (p. 30). The narrator's problem is
clear. Saniette and the clerk are so sophisticated that they
can understand nothing. Only when his motives are glibly
and irrelevantly identified with a familiar sexual aberra-
tion can he get a hearing for them. And Saniette's "cooper-
ative" response is therefore insulting. It denies the reality of
his feelings. The Pamphlet concludes with a bitter and
appropriate comment:

> Saniette represents a distinct type of audience—smart,
> sophisticated, sensitive yet hardboiled, art-loving frequent-
> ers of the little theatres. I am their particular kind of
> performer.
> Some day I shall obtain my revenge by writing a play
> for one of their art theatres. . . .
> In this play I shall take my beloved patrons into my
> confidence and flatter their good taste in preferring Art to
> animal acts. Then, suddenly, in the midst of some very
> witty dialogue, the entire cast will walk to the footlights
> and shout Chekhov's advice:
> "It would be more profitable for the farmer to raise rats
> for the granary than for the bourgeois to nourish the
> artist, who must always be occupied with undermining
> institutions."

In case the audience should misunderstand and align
itself on the side of the artist, the ceiling of the theatre will
be made to open and cover the occupants with tons of
loose excrement. After the deluge, if they so desire, the
patrons of my art can gather in the customary charming
groups and discuss the play. (Pp. 30–31.)

Even if we accept the narrator's statement that "All my
acting has but one purpose, the attraction of the female" (p.
26), we cannot reduce the Pamphlet to Gilson's terms. The
narrator's description of the "chaffeur within" portrays sex
as a dirty and joyless compulsion. He obviously resents the
compulsion as much as he resents the poses he must adopt to
gratify it. Indeed, Saniette seems quite willing to satisfy the
"chaffeur within," but to satisfy the "chaffeur" is not to
satisfy the narrator.

Like the Journal, the Pamphlet presents a narrator who is
an actor in a double sense: he indulges in theatrical poses
and in acts of violence. His motives for both kinds of act
are simultaneously compulsive and literary. He is quite unable to escape this confusion of motives; his most sincere
expressions have an air of imposture, and his most deliberate
poses an element of compulsion. The whole Gilson section
—Journal, Pamphlet, and dialogue with Balso—reads like
the work of a man who is equally embarrassed by the fakery
of his sufferings and by their reality, and who hides both
embarrassments by pretending that the fake is deliberate
and total.

This last remark is, however, dangerously solemn, especially since it is applied to a work whose prevailing tone is
farce. Much of the Gilson section is accurate and funny
parody of familiar arty stances. It also contains, of course,
several themes which figure prominently in West's later

novels. Saniette is an early version of the uncomprehending nice girl—of the Betty in *Miss Lonelyhearts.* The "natural antipathy" of "pessimists . . . for optimists" is simply West's paraphrase of William James's contrast between "morbid-mindedness" and "healthy-mindedness." James cites the "Mind-Cure movement" as one form of the "religion of healthy-mindedness,"[21] and Saniette appropriately relies on "Mother Eddy and Doctor Coué." The "equally natural antipathy felt by the performer for his audience"(p. 25) is omnipresent in West's work, notably in *The Day of the Locust.* The idiot's masklike face, the opera singer's laugh, the botched and terrible throat cutting, the compulsion to attain order, the inescapability of imposture, obscure irritation, "unmotivated" violence—all reappear in the later books. And Gilson's Journal foreshadows another characteristic West device: treating a Dostoevskian subject in a French style.

As Gilson disappears, pure farce and fatuity reappear. So do the ghosts of Huysmans and Cabell. Balso sees a naked girl "washing her hidden charms in a public fountain" (p. 31), but when he embraces her, she turns middle-aged and tweed-covered in his arms. The incident recalls, as I have already said, Jurgen's similar experience with Dorothea, but the echoes do not end there. The woman is Gilson's teacher, Miss McGeeney, and she is a comprehensive anthology of literary clichés. She moves from the nonsense of book reviewers—"Stark, clever, disillusioned stuff, with a tender-

---

[21] William James, *The Varieties of Religious Experience,* p. 93. For a more complete discussion of West's borrowings from James, see Chapter III, below. Saniette is also, like the Bergotte quoted on the title page, a character in *Remembrance of Things Past.* In Proust, the character is male, a member of the Verdurin circle whose naïve and inept niceness invites the malice of others.

ness devoid of sentiment, yet touched by pity and laughter
and irony" (p. 32)—to the pendantry of scholarly para-
sites—she is writing a biography of the man who wrote a
biography of the man who wrote a biography of the man
who wrote a biography of the man who wrote a biography
of Samuel Johnson—to the perverse and extravagant artiness
of the symbolist-decadent tradition.

> "He had found in the odors of a woman's body, never-
> ending, ever-fresh variation and change—a world of
> dreams, seas, roads, forests, textures, colors, flavors, forms.
> . . . He told me that he had built from the odors of his
> wife's body an architecture and an aesthetic, a music and a
> mathematic. Counterpoint, multiplication, the square of a
> sensation, the cube root of an experience—all were there.
> He told me that he had even discovered a politic, a hierar-
> chy of odors: self-government, direct . . ." (P. 36.)

One can go from this to Huysmans' *Against the Grain*
without even the discomfort of a noticeable transition.

> He held that the sense of smell was qualified to experience
> pleasures equal to those pertaining to the ear and the eye,
> each of the five senses being capable, by dint of a natural
> aptitude supplemented by an erudite education, of receiv-
> ing novel impressions, magnifying these tenfold, coordi-
> nating them, combining them into the whole that consti-
> tutes a work of art. . . .
>   To reach this end, he had, first of all, been obliged to
> master the grammar, to understand the syntax of
> odours. . . .[22]

Huysmans is full of such stuff; in his "Le Gousset," as Have-
lock Ellis said, "the capacities of language are strained to de-

---

[22] Huysmans' *Against the Grain*, pp. 216 and 218. Huysmans' similar
experiments with the sense of taste are specifically mentioned in this
passage of *Balso Snell*.

fine and differentiate the odours of feminine arm-pits."[23]
And Huysmans seems to be lurking in the wings whenever
Miss McGeeney appears on stage. Her invitation to Balso
lovingly catalogues "the protuberances on the skin of
streets—warts, tumours, pimples, corns, nipples, sebaceous
cysts, hard and soft chancres" and describes a pleasure
garden where "like the gums of false teeth, red are the signs
imploring you to enter the game paths lit by iron flowers"
(p. 32). And Balso recalls that the youthful Miss Mc-
Geeney "did nothing but place bits of meat on the petals
of flowers. She choked the rose with butter and cake
crumbs, soiling the crispness of its dainty petals with gravy
and cheese. She wanted the rose to attract flies, not butter-
flies or bees." (P. 57.) Fascination with the artificial, the
perverse, and the unpleasantly anatomical was always typical of Huysmans. His hero, Des Esseintes, held that "artifice was . . . the distinctive mark of human genius,"[24] and
collected exotic plants which "mimicked zinc, parodied
pieces of stencilled metal coloured emperor-green" or dis-
played "livid patches of flesh, reddened by measles, rough-
ened by eruptions" or "showed the bright pink of a half-
closed wound" or "offered hairy surfaces eaten into holes
by ulcers and excavated by chancres."[25] And Des Esseintes
even remembered a former mistress who "loved to have her
nipples macerated in scents, but who only really experienced a genuine and overmastering ecstasy when her head
was tickled with a comb and she could, in the act of being
caressed by a lover, breathe the smell of chimney
soot. . . ."[26] Once again, the parody is, of course, generic

[23] Ellis, Introduction to *Against the Grain*, p. 30.
[24] *Against the Grain*, p. 103.
[25] *Ibid.*, p. 188.
[26] *Ibid.*, p. 226.

as well as specific; it extends to many of the symbolists who preceded Huysmans and to the decadents who followed him.

In the Janey Davenport–Beagle Darwin sequence, the prevailing farce undergoes a spasm of comic metamorphosis and illusion. Janey's death and Beagle's lament are both imaginary events, the literary invention of Beagle Darwin, a man who describes himself as so "deeply dyed" by literature that it is impossible for him to tell where literature ends and he begins. Further, Beagle's invention is a part of Balso's dream, which is in turn a part of the general dream of the novel. We have, then, an imaginary lament over an imaginary death occurring in a dream within a dream. But even this is too simple. Balso awakens to discover that perhaps he only imagined that he dreamed he dreamed—Beagle's letters were actually written by that tireless literary status seeker, Miss McGeeney. At this point, a critic may find himself echoing John Gilson: "Reality! Reality! If I could only discover the Real!" (p. 14). The obvious point is that we can't. The multiple illusions allow but one conclusion: the world of art is so consumed by pretentious fakery that even its suffering is literary and false.

If, however, we keep that point firmly in mind, we can allow ourselves a few additional observations. Beagle's evocation of Janey's thoughts involves a new kind of parody —that of ordinary, non-literary triteness. Though Janey has picked up a few arty phrases, her clichés are largely those of a nice, not very intellectual American girl.

> Since my father's death, I have no one to go to with my misery. He was always willing to understand and comfort me. Oh, how I want to be understood by someone who really loves me. (P. 42.)

He is like all men; he wants only one thing (p. 44).
What love and a child by the man I loved once meant to
me—and to live in Paris (p. 46).

And Janey sometimes rises above triteness—"death is like
putting on a wet bathing suit" (p. 44)—or transforms triteness by the force of real emotion. " 'I'm serious! I am! I am!
I don't want to live! I'm miserable! I don't want to live!' "
(P. 46.) If we ignore the farcical context, Janey's thoughts
are, despite their triteness, convincing and somewhat moving. There is another new element in this parody: the
juxtaposition of the naïve with the sophisticated, of the
emotional girl with the mocking male, of Janey with
Beagle. Janey is, like Saniette, an early version of Miss
Lonelyhearts' Betty, and Beagle is an obvious ancestor of
Shrike. Like Shrike, he is an actor. He speaks an elaborate
comic rhetoric composed of literary and vulgar clichés.

> "Or quick tell me where has gone Samson?—strongest
> of men. He is no longer even weak. And where, oh tell
> me, where is the beautiful Appollon? He is no longer even
> ugly. And where are the snows of yesteryear? And where
> is Tom Giles? Bill Taylor? Jake Holtz? In other words,
> 'Here today and gone tomorrow.' " (P. 54.)

Though the playlet Beagle stages may glance at the
Nighttown scene in *Ulysses*,[27] it has a far more obvious
source: Greek tragedy. It features a messenger and a
chorus, and Beagle even borrows his invocation of

---

[27] Light quotes I. J. Kapstein, a college friend of West's, as saying that
the *Walpurgisnacht* scene from *Ulysses* was the "major influence on *The
Dream Life*" (p. 41). Kapstein' opinion carries the authority of personal
acquaintance with West, and it is also supported by the obvious echoes
of Joyce in *Balso Snell*. I do not, however, think the *Walpurgisnacht*
influence is as strong as that of Huysmans and Cabell.

Dionysus—" 'Bromius! Iacchus! Son of Zeus!' " (p. 53)—
from *The Bacchae*. The source is of more than incidental
interest. West wrote an essay on Euripides for his college
literary magazine,[28] and the influence of Greek tragedy in
general and Euripides in particular shows throughout his
work. His use of masks, of ritual gesture, of mythic themes,
of dramatic irony, of symbolic violence, and of highly
formal and condensed rhetoric can be traced in part to the
Greek drama. And the satiric, iconoclastic portrayal of
gods and heroes which he found in Euripides obviously
appealed to him. Even Beagle's "spiritual Darwinism," with
its ironic description of the unfair competition between
gods and mortals, resembles the Euripidean vision of the
gods.

Another influence, barely visible here, appears more
clearly in West's later treatment of Shrike. We know from
the reminiscences of John Sanford that West was fond of
Huxley's *Antic Hay*,[29] and we also know that he liked to
quote Odo of Cluny's definition of woman as *saccus
stercoris*.[30] He probably picked up the quotation by reading
Huxley, not by reading the fathers of the Church. The
"satanic" Coleman of *Antic Hay* cities Odo of Cluny, and
he also spouts the "O esca vermium! O massa pulveris"
which Beagle quotes in his playlet.[31] And Coleman is, like
Beagle and like Shrike, addicted to a stagey, mock-

[28] Light, p. 30. Light says that West praised Euripides' writing "in its
fusion of the satirist with the man of feeling," and he suggests that West
attempted a similar fusion in his own work. I do not think the influence
was limited merely to a general attitude.

[29] *Ibid.*, pp. 63–64.

[30] *Ibid.*, p. 24.

[31] Huxley, *Antic Hay and The Giaconda Smile*, p. 216. See also note
21, Chapter III, below.

grandiloquent rhetoric. Apart from some echoes in Miss McGeeney's seduction responses, West's adaptations of Huxley are, however, neither as important nor as skillful here as they are in *Miss Lonelyhearts*.

Catharsis

In the final episode of *Balso Snell*, nothing intrudes upon the sublime fatuousness of Balso and Miss McGeeney. The guide, Maloney the Areopagite, John Gilson, Janey Davenport, and Beagle Darwin have all disappeared. So have all distracting metamorphoses. With Miss McGeeney lying flat on her back, her knees spread, Balso launches into a series of highly conventional and totally unnecessary seduction speeches. And of course he is answered by all the conventional responses—Miss McGeeney is indeed a comprehensive anthology of clichés. The responses predictably move from a maidenly no to a Joycean yes; there is the moment of orgasmic release; and then the "army that a moment before had been thundering in [Balso's] body retreated slowly—victorious, relieved" (p. 62). This is the "climax" of the novel—a wet dream. And it is a climax in the literary sense as well. The three main themes of the novel—art, dreams, sex—are here united in simultaneous and triumphant parody.

Perhaps now we should introduce the usual naïve question: but what does it all mean? It "means," of course, that a good many fashionable ideas and stances have been made ridiculous through parody. Let us sum them up:

The dream.—The surrealists held that dreams were a visionary revelation, a creative perception whose enemy was reason, consciousness, custom. In Balso's dream, however, the unconscious is as derivative as the conscious.

There is no mystic revelation, only a medley of arty clichés. The Freudian dream theory is equally ridiculous and for much the same reason. It is Balso's reading, not his neurosis, which determines the symbols of his dream. His fantasies just express and gratify the psychiatrically meaningless fact of his tumescence. The Cabellian dream, with its mixture of irony and nostalgia, is ridiculed by the various scatological devices I have already described. And Jurgen's "philosophic" resignation after his erotic adventures is also parodied by Balso's meaningless peace after his meaningless orgasm.

Sex.—The various episodes in *Balso Snell* amount to a catalogue of sexual attitudes, traditional and contemporary: sex as the devil in the flesh (Huysmans and Christian mysticism), as romantic ecstasy (*carpe diem* poetry), as grand passion (movies and magazines), as rational pleasure (Bertrand Russell), as dark compulsion (Dostoevski), as sensual mystery (D. H. Lawrence), as root of all motives (Freud), and as the occasion for a lyrical display of language (James Joyce). These various attitudes seem equally pretentious and equally ridiculous when compared to Balso's orgasm. They are all ways of imputing meaning to an experience which has none. Balso's ecstasy is simply "an eager army of hurrying sensations" (p. 61) which performs its "long intricate drill" with "the confidence and training of chemicals acting under the stimulus of a catalytic agent" (p. 62). It is "like the mechanics of decay" (p. 61).

Art.—All artistic poses are, in the final scene, reduced to seduction strategies. Gilson's thesis seems hilariously confirmed—the only purpose of art is to disguise and gratify sexual desire. Yet it is equally true that sex seems largely an excuse to indulge in arty poses. Though Miss McGeeney flops down and immediately spreads her knees, both she and Balso tune up and run through their repertoires before getting down to business. Balso is simultaneously a lecher disguised as an artist and a ham disguised as a lecher. The fraud is thereby total. Imposture is not just a disguise for his real motives because Balso has no real motives: imposture is his essence.

Several questions remain. I have argued, for example, that the "scatology" of *Balso Snell* is an intricate and fundamental joke, not just a willful dabbling in filth. But is the joke a good one? Those to whom the indecent is automatically offensive—or, even worse, automatically grounds for clinical speculation—will have their own answer. I think the joke is both legitimate and funny. But I also think that West's execution of it is sometimes strained and unfunny, especially in the first ten or twelve pages. Why? Perhaps the joke is too good, the sort of bright idea which seduces its originator into endlessly elaborating his own cleverness. Yet the joke really suffers less from over-elaboration than from clumsy attempts at low comedy. In the opening pages, West seems to wobble between the Rabelaisian and the Aristophanic, and he was not good at either style. Balso's parody of the epic catalogue and his spasm of arty name dropping with the guide need a Rabelaisian zest to be funny, but there is little real zest in these pages. The sense of inexhaustible energy which makes each additional detail in Rabelais funnier than the last—funnier because it is additional and because there seems no end to the additions—is almost totally absent in West. His talent was hardly volcanic. And he was as bad at simple clowning as he was at playing Gargantua. The Aristophanic buffooneries of Balso's "Stinker!" and of his violent wrestlings with the guide are just depressing.

There is, of course, a biographical fact which may explain the unevenness of *Balso Snell*. The first draft was written in 1924 when West was still in college, but the

manuscript was not published until 1931.[32] To conclude
that the "juvenile" portions are relics of the undergraduate
version and that the "mature" portions were written or
rewritten later is both tempting and natural. It is not, however, entirely satisfactory. West was a notoriously careful
writer. If his taste and talent had undergone so distinct a
change, why did he not revise the whole manuscript before
publishing it? And why did he again lapse into unsubtle and
frequently unfunny humor in *A Cool Million*? Such questions obviously have no sure answers. A writer's talents are
subject to the same lapses that other human qualities are,
and we cannot pretend to know why. A few observations,
however, seem definitely relevant.

Low comedy may have attracted West precisely because
he was not good at it. The kind of perception which in-
forms *Miss Lonelyhearts* and *The Day of the Locust*
makes any simple response impossible, and such perception
is a burden, especially when, as seems true of West, it is as
involuntary as sight itself. West automatically noticed both
the awkward sham in a heroic gesture and the grimace of
real pain in a pratfall. There is little to laugh at in either
case. Both the gesture and the pratfall are unsuccessful acts,
and both are ultimately depressing in the way that all failure is. Given such a vision, simple laughter can become as
appealing as affirmative belief—and as difficult to attain. In
West's novels, something always happens to make belief
ridiculous or to make laughter sag. For him, the role of
triumphant comedian was an unsuccessful impersonation.

Instinctive pessimism is not, however, all that is responsible for the failure of West's broad comedy. He seems to

[32] Light, p. 31.

have lacked the necessary ease. Physical exuberance is fundamental to horseplay, but West's central characters are typically deadened and constricted. They are incapable of fluid motion. When they witness it in others—as in the dance between Faye and Miguel in *The Day of the Locust*—it appears mindless, alien, enviable, and threatening. When they attempt it themselves, it appears strained. West's own clowning in *Balso Snell* seems equally strained. Only when he abandons physical buffoonery for verbal parody—as in Miss McGeeney's seduction responses—does his performance become assured and hilarious. And even then his success depends upon the cool precision of each phrase, not on an exuberant display of energy.

It also depends upon the radical compression of language. Miss McGeeney's responses are not quoted. Instead, they are given a summary paraphrase which reveals the essence of each pose with all the economy of an epigram. Unlike an epigram, however, the paraphrase is formed from the vocabulary natural to the imposture. It is parody, but parody reduced to the concentration of poetry. And the distilled paraphrase thereby becomes a generic expression, the revelation of a classic attitude or response to life, not just a caricature of a particular model. It combines the verisimilitude of actual speech with the economy and lucidity of comment.

Some elements in *Balso Snell* are, however, simply mistakes. West often sacrifices parody for the sake of a wisecrack. Maloney the Areopagite says of St. Puce: " 'Like most of us, he had two fathers: Our Father Who art in Heaven, and he who in the cocksureness of our youth we called "pop" ' " (p. 11). The last phrase is, of course, totally inappropriate to Maloney. It is also totally appropriate to Beagle Darwin—or to the later rhetoric of Shrike. Apparently West had not yet finished sorting out the voices in his head.

A final observation is necessary. Though in *Balso Snell* ridicule seems total, it is directed less at art in general than at certain forms of pseudo-art—at the derivative, the pretentious, the fashionable. *Balso's* characters are would-be writers and intellectuals. They pretend to originality but succeed only in mimicking familiar stances. Even when they are aware of it—as John Gilson and Beagle Darwin are—they are unable to escape imitation. For such characters, parody is a way of life, at times almost a fate. And the fate is not necessarily funny. In *Balso Snell*, West began to explore both the possibilities in parody as a literary technique and the implications of parody as a human problem. *Miss Lonelyhearts* represents, among other things, the natural result of those explorations.

Miss Lonelyhearts:
THE DEAD REDEEMER

The mockery which was pervasive in *Balso Snell* has, in *Miss Lonelyhearts*, shrunk to the person of Shrike, supported by a chorus of largely anonymous newspapermen. Miss Lonelyhearts himself is a man who has "learned not to laugh,"[1] a man for whom the joke of fraudulent salvation is "no longer funny" (p. 12). This change is matched, perhaps caused, by the introduction of a new class of sufferers—the desperate and semi-literate writers of letters to Miss Lonelyhearts. Where the Trojan horse of *Balso Snell* was peopled entirely by camp-followers of the arts, the world of *Miss Lonelyhearts* includes humbler victims of a more serious misery. The sixteen-year-old girl who was born without a nose, the brother of the idiot girl who has been raped and made pregnant by an unknown man, and the mother who signs herself "Sick-of-It-All" are all victims of a misery not caused by literary pretensions. They are the victims of life, of biological defects compounded by the cruelty of their fellows. Their letters are trite, illiterate, and sentimental,

---

[1] *Miss Lonelyhearts* (New York: New Direction, n.d.), p. 87. Subsequent references are to the same edition and are indicated by page numbers in parentheses.

but the misery which they reveal cannot be doubted, nor does anyone in the novel seriously doubt it. Even Shrike's mockery serves to emphasize, rather than to destroy, the seriousness of human misery. Miss Lonelyhearts insists that misery requires a solution, that the pain inevitably associated with life is both real and unbearable. Shrike insists that a solution is impossible and that human aspirations are absurd. Both attitudes receive dramatic confirmation in the novel. When Miss Farkis tries to be intellectual, she is only silly. When Mary Shrike tries to be glamorous, she is an absurdly transparent actress. Yet when Miss Lonelyhearts tries to be funny, as in the episode of the clean old man, he blunders into violence. The sacrifice of the lamb starts as a college prank and ends in terror. Mary Shrike wants to be gay, but she can only lapse into a monotonous recitation of her mother's suffering. When West's people try to be serious, they are ridiculous; when they try to be funny, they are frightening. Thus the dual vision of the novel yields a precise statement about its characters: despite their pretensions, their pain is real. And their absurdity in no way lessens the importance of their pain. Rather, it is a symptom of it. Squalid suffering is an evil precisely because it destroys all dignity, not just because it hurts.

Both pretense and pain are associated with sexuality. The newspapermen who function as a chorus for Shrike echo a familiar refrain from *Balso Snell*—that art is just a disguise for the procreative urge. Miss Lonelyhearts overhears them telling a series of stories about lady writers to prove that "what they all needed was a good rape."[2] He observes:

---

[2] This scene appears to include some self-criticism. Light quotes John Sanford's reminiscences of West in the New York years which preceded *Miss Lonelyhearts:* "'He hated loud talk . . . three-name women writers (Thyra Samter Winslow, Viola Brothers Shore). . . .'" Light, p. 63.

His friends would go on telling these stories until they were too drunk to talk. They were aware of their child-ishness, but did not know how else to revenge themselves. At college, and perhaps for a year afterwards, they had believed in literature, had believed in Beauty and in per-sonal expression as an absolute end. When they lost this belief, they lost everything. . . . They were not worldly men. (P. 61.)

For Miss Lonelyhearts, sex may be a compulsion, but it is no kind of cure. Both his own sexual adventures and those of the other characters are peculiarly joyless and repellent. With Mrs. Doyle, the very personification of the life force, Miss Lonelyhearts feels "like an empty bottle that is being slowly filled with warm, dirty water" (p. 184). The "water" is, of course, a symbol of sexual desire and the natural world from which it comes, a world which is repre-sented throughout the novel by the conventional metaphor of the sea. Miss Lonelyhearts tries in fantasy to create order out of all the junk deposited by the sea, and when he goes to bed with Mrs. Doyle the entire seduction is described in sea metaphors.

He smoked a cigarette, standing in the dark and listen-ing to her undress. She made sea sounds; something flapped like a sail; there was the creak of ropes; then he heard the wave-against-a-wharf smack of rubber on flesh. Her call for him to hurry was a sea-moan, and when he lay beside her, she heaved, tidal, moon-driven.

Some fifteen minutes later, he crawled out of bed like an exhausted swimmer leaving the surf. . . . (P. 107.)

The description is at once hilarious and terrible, for West characteristically exploits both the comic and the thematic possibilities of his metaphor. The thematic possibilities are relentless in their implication. Miss Lonelyhearts regards Doyle as the test of his mission; his attempt to save Doyle is an attempt to save all the letter writers, and, significantly, he is defeated by the "tidal, moon-driven" Mrs. Doyle, by the life force itself.

The destructiveness of sex is not the only theme from *Balso Snell* to be echoed in *Miss Lonelyhearts*. Art, dreams, and imposture are as omnipresent as ever. So is parody. Shrike's rehearsal of all the classic forms of escape is exactly like Miss McGeeney's rehearsal of all the classic responses to seduction—it defines and destroys the available alternatives. And the parody does not end with Shrike's targets. It extends to Shrike himself—a cartoon of a satirist whose every gesture is artificial and whose stance is as derivative as it is destructive. Thus satire is, in the person of Shrike, satirized, and mockery is thereby disqualified as an adequate response to human misery. Nor do the uses of parody and pastiche end here. West's synthesis of borrowed material is, in *Miss Lonelyhearts*, so skillful that it is often unnoticed and so original that it has the effect of novelty. Dashiell Hammett's comment—"A new note in American writing; in his work there are no echoes of other men's books"[3]—would be echoed by many readers of *Miss Lonelyhearts*. It has the paradoxical merit of being both accurate and absurd. Hammett was hardly fatuous, of course, and his statement is as true in the sense that he intended as it is false in another. West was not a derivative writer. And he did indeed sound a new note in American writing, but it was a note largely compounded from the echoes of a great many books.

Varieties of Religious Experience

How irrelevantly remote seem all our usual refined optimisms and intellectual and moral consolations in presence

[3] Quoted in an advertisement for *Miss Lonelyhearts* in *Contempo*, III (July 25, 1933), 7.

of a need of help like this! Here is the real core of the
religious problem: Help! Help! No prophet can claim to
bring a final message unless he says things that will have a
sound of reality in the ears of victims such as these.—
William James [4]

The victims James speaks of are sufferers from insane
melancholia, but his description of them and of the "real
core of the religious problem" is so appropriate to *Miss
Lonelyhearts* that it sounds like an epigraph written to
order. The relevance is not coincidental. In "Some Notes
on Miss Lonelyhearts," West said:

> Miss Lonelyhearts became the portrait of a priest of our
> time who has a religious experience. His case is classical
> and is built on all the cases in James' *Varieties of Religious
> Experience* and Starbuck's *Psychology of Religion*. The
> psychology is theirs not mine. The immagery [*sic*] is
> mine. [5]

These remarks are not definitive—there is a more important
source for West's psychology than either James or Starbuck—but they do establish that West knew *The Varieties
of Religious Experience* and that he had it in mind when
working on *Miss Lonelyhearts*. *Miss Lonelyhearts* itself
shows in what ways he had it in mind.

Except for one or two details, West does not seem to
have borrowed from any particular case cited by James or
Starbuck. [6] Instead, he focuses on the classic states which

[4] William James, p. 159.
[5] West, "Some Notes on Miss Lonelyhearts," pp. 1–2.
[6] The details are both trivial and uncertain. I will cite one example.
James quotes C. G. Finney: "After this distinct revelation had stood for
some little time before my mind, the question seemed to be put, 'Will
you accept it now, to-day?' I replied 'Yes; I will accept it today, or I
will die in the attempt.' " (P. 204.) At the moment of Miss Lonelyhearts'
union with God, a similar question is heard: "God said, 'Will you accept
it now?' And he replied, 'I accept, I accept.' " (P. 211.)

precede conversion—deadness, disorder, self-conscious sin-
ning, attempted flight from God, despair, and final submission. There is, however, an important distinction between
Miss Lonelyhearts' case and the classic pattern. It is not the
sense of his own sin, or the terror of his own damnation, or
the sudden perception of God's beauty and benevolence
which moves him. Rather, it is the misery of others. He
plays at being a redeemer, not a saint. He does not, as
Bunyan did, start with the absolute conviction of God's
reality and then struggle to mend his own weakness. Instead, he starts with the perception that human misery demands a divine answer and then tries to convince himself
that such an answer exists. He tries to invoke God in this
life, to redeem, to revivify. His fate parodies the heroic
quest, not the pilgrimage.[7]

The logic of Miss Lonelyhearts' quest owes, in other
words, as much to James's philosophical analysis as to his
psychology. The "real core of the religious problem," said
James, is "Help! Help!"—and of course Chapter I of *Miss
Lonelyhearts* is headed: "Miss Lonelyhearts, help me, help
me." Nor is this the only point at which James touches the
novel's themes. His fundamental contrast between "morbid-mindedness" and "healthy-mindedness" is at least as
important to the psychology of Miss Lonelyhearts as are
the Lives of the Saints. In *Balso Snell*, this contrast appears
in the "natural antipathy" of pessimists for optimists, in the
conflict between Gilson's narrator and Saniette. It is ex-

[7] The theme of the quest has been emphasized by Light, who connects it with West's Jewishness, and by Comerchero, who constructs
extended parallels between *Miss Lonelyhearts* and the analyses of grail
legend and heroic myth offered by Jessie L. Weston and Joseph Campbell.
See Light, pp. 135–36, and Comerchero, pp. 86–94.

pressed even more clearly in the conflict between Miss
Lonelyhearts and Betty. James says:

> Systematic healthy-mindedness, conceiving good as the
> essential and universal aspect of being, deliberately ex-
> cludes evil from its field of vision. . . .[8]
> To . . . the morbid-minded way, as we might call it,
> healthy-mindedness pure and simple seems unspeakably
> blind and shallow.[9]

We are bound to say that morbid-mindedness ranges
over the wider scale of experience, and that its survey is
the one that overlaps. . . . There is no doubt that
healthy-mindedness is inadequate as a philosophical doctrine, because the evil facts which it refuses positively to
account for are a genuine portion of reality; and they may
after all be the best key to life's significance, and possibly
the only openers of our eyes to the deepest levels of
truth.[10]

Miss Lonelyhearts' comments on Betty are a succinct paraphrase of James's remarks.

> Her world was not the world and could never include the
> readers of his column. Her sureness was based on the
> power to limit experience arbitrarily. Moreover, his con-
> fusion was significant, while her order was not. (Pp.
> 49–50).

"Morbid-mindedness" and "healthy-mindedness," as James
describes them, are obviously not just temperamental pecu-
liarities to be classified by the clinical psychologist. They

---

[8] James, pp. 86–87. Among others, Daniel Aaron has briefly discussed
the influence of James, mentioning especially the contrast between
"healthy-mindedness" and the "sick soul." Aaron also attributes—mistakenly, I think—the structure of *Miss Lonelyhearts* to *The Varieties of
Religious Experience*. See Aaron, "Late Thoughts on Nathanael West."

[9] James, p. 159.

[10] *Ibid.*, p. 160.

are instead conflicting religious and philosophical attitudes toward the nature of life. They divide sharply on the problem of evil. To the morbid-minded, evil is fundamental and ineradicable. To the healthy-minded, evil is either illusory or minor and transient. Miss Lonelyhearts and Betty exhibit this polarity of attitudes in all its forms. James identified love of nature as one characteristic of the religion of healthy-mindedness (he mentions Whitman as an example),[11] and of course Betty asserts that all Miss Lonelyhearts' troubles are "city troubles." To cure him, she takes him first to the zoo and then to the country. The concept of cure is itself fundamental to healthy-mindedness. Because nature is good and life is happy, evil and misery must be "unnatural." They are illnesses to be treated, temporary disorders in a basically healthy organism. Betty insists on regarding all evil as a problem in mental and physical hygiene, with "nature" as the panacea. Miss Lonelyhearts says: "As soon as any one acts viciously, you say he's sick. Wife-torturers, rapers of small children, according to you they're all sick. No morality, only medicine." (P. 53.)

At least in its more extreme and typically American forms, the religion of healthy-mindedness is, as James noted, an inversion of traditional Christian doctrine. It denies sin, views nature as idyllic, and makes redemption unnecessary. Eden is our birthright, and goodness is our natural condition. To Miss Lonelyhearts, however, nature is inherently evil. Its "tropism for disorder, entropy" is eloquently confirmed by the letters. Though morbid-mindedness may be pathological, it is also virtually irrefutable. Even the normally sanguine James observed:

[11] *Ibid.*, p. 83.

The lunatic's visions of horror are all drawn from the material of daily fact. Our civilization is founded on the shambles, and every individual existence goes out in a lonely spasm of helpless agony.[12]

And again:

We divert our attention from disease and death as much as we can; and the slaughter-houses and indecencies without end on which our life is founded are huddled out of sight and never mentioned, so that the world we recognize officially in literature and in society is a poetic fiction far handsomer and cleaner and better than the world that really is.[13]

Miss Lonelyhearts is, of course, a man who can no longer divert his attention. The letters themselves are a fatal intrusion upon that "poetic fiction [we] recognize officially in literature and in society." They have the vividness and the unarguable reality of a revelation. William Carlos Williams, in his review of *Miss Lonelyhearts*, testified to their veracity.

The letters which West uses freely and at length must be authentic. I can't believe anything else. The unsuspected world they reveal is beyond ordinary thought. . . . Should such lives as these letters reveal never have been brought to light? Should such people, like the worst of our war wounded, best be kept in hiding?[14]

The strategy of the novel is exactly to reveal that "unsuspected world," to reveal it so clearly that our usual response—ignore it—is no longer possible. The strategy is as appalling as it is simple. In a world where evil and unre-

[12] *Ibid.*, p. 160.
[13] *Ibid.*, p. 89.
[14] William Carlos Williams, "Sordid? Good God!" p. 5.

lieved suffering are everywhere, redemption is an absolute
need. There is no other answer to the cry for help. And in
West's vision, that means there is no answer at all. As the
letters reveal, the "real core of the religious problem" continues even when religions die. "Enlightenment" only ag-
gravates the problem. For "victims such as these," if God is
dead, so is hope.

Dostoevski with a Pair of Shears

The general influence of Dostoevski on West's work is
obvious. It was noted by Angel Flores in his 1933 review of
Miss Lonelyhearts,[15] and it has been mentioned again in
nearly every succeeding commentary on West. As these
studies have pointed out, West was, like Dostoevski, fond
of treating guilt-ridden, dualistic characters who live and
act in a strangely hallucinatory world.[16] But the influence is
not limited to this general resemblance. John Sanford has
recalled West's "little brag that he could rewrite
Dostoevsky with a pair of shears,"[17] and in *Miss Lonelyhearts* that is very nearly what West did. He took his
structure, and the psychology which underlies the structure, intact from *Crime and Punishment*. The case history
of Raskolnikov was far more useful to him than any he
found in James or Starbuck.

Both Raskolnikov and Miss Lonelyhearts are, when we
meet them, already launched on an obsessive idea whose

---

[15] Flores, p. 1.

[16] James Light, for example, has repeatedly mentioned Dostoevski in
connection with West, but he has not attempted any systematic examination of West's borrowings from *Crime and Punishment*. See especially
Light, "Violence, Dreams, and Dostoevsky: The Art of Nathanael West,"
pp. 208–13.

[17] John Sanford, "Nathanael West," p. 13.

genesis is only hinted at. In both, the obsession ambiguously reflects a personal illness and a real external problem—it is simultaneously true that Miss Lonelyhearts is driven by "hysteria" and that he is driven by a clear perception of the misery of others, just as it is true that Raskolnikov is driven by a treacherous combination of pathological motives and real perceptions. In both cases, the external problem is the fact of apparently hopeless suffering. And in both cases, the resulting obsession focuses on the necessity of an heroic action—Raskolnikov imitates Napoleon; Miss Lonelyhearts imitates Christ. The heroic action raises a series of questions: Is the action desirable? Is the hero capable of it? Are his apparent motives real? Raskolnikov and Miss Lonelyhearts alternately doubt the action itself and their own worthiness to attempt it. Even their failures are ambiguous. Has the ideal failed, or has the hero failed his ideal?

Apart from their internal doubts, both Raskolnikov and Miss Lonelyhearts face two kinds of external opposition: cynical mockery and naïve orthodoxy. Porfiry Petrovitch and Svidrigailov mock Raskolnikov's attempt to play Superman; Shrike mocks Miss Lonelyhearts' attempt to play Christ. Sonia's orthodox Christianity is horrified by murder and godlessness; Betty's orthodox Americanism is repelled by misery and martyrdom. Both Raskolnikov and Miss Lonelyhearts are, in other words, poised between mocking antagonists and loving but incomprehending girls. Each attempts to resist the mockery and to destroy the simple faith: Raskolnikov invades Sonia's room to insist that all her sacrifice is futile, that only shame and suffering await her and the children she is trying to protect; Miss Lonelyhearts invades Betty's apartment to smash her Buddha-like serenity and insist on the reality of evil. Both resent a composure which seems to deny the heroic roles they have chosen. These parallels yield several satiric points. Sonia and Betty embody paradoxes: Sonia is the saintly whore whose spiritual purity contrasts with her physical degradation; Betty is the nice girl whose innocence is a form of corruption. When American orthodoxy replaces Russian orthodoxy, veneration of nature and success replaces veneration of love and sacrifice. Instead of "Take up your cross," Betty's advice is: Go into advertising.

Crime and Punishment also uses three narrative devices which West adopted: the set speech, the confession, and the dream. Both *Crime and Punishment* and *Miss Lonelyhearts* contain little true dialogue. Raskolnikov and Miss Lonelyhearts do not talk much, except to themselves. They are usually silent auditors for the extended and formal speech of others. Raskolnikov listens to Marmeladov, to Razumihin, to Porfiry Petrovitch, to Svidrigailov; Miss Lonelyhearts listens to Shrike, to Mary Shrike, to Mrs. Doyle. These extended speeches often seem, in both novels, simultaneously theatrical and natural. They sound rehearsed, but that is the way they ought to sound. The habitual confider (Marmeladov and Mary Shrike) is, after all, an actor. His tale of woe is a recital—the repetition of a story told so often that it is nearly memorized. And acting is the natural posture of seducers, detectives, and intellectuals. Svidrigailov, Porfiry Petrovitch, and Shrike are all self-conscious actors who deliberately exploit the artificiality of their roles; Shrike is the sort who fabricates his speeches in advance, hoarding every epigram which occurs to him. Both novels largely substitute the conventions of stage speech—soliloquy and monologue—for ordinary conversation, but both novels make this stage speech plausible by using self-conscious and self-dramatizing characters.

The confession—bogus and real—is also omnipresent in both novels. Raskolnikov hears the confessions of Marmeladov, Svidrigailov, and Porfiry Petrovitch; Miss Lonelyhearts receives endless confessional letters and hears the troubles of Mary Shrike and Mrs. Doyle. The confession is, of course, one form of the monologue or set speech. It also defines the auditor in curious ways. If confessing is a theatrical role, so is playing confessor, and both Raskolnikov and Miss Lonelyhearts are tormented in part by the implications of their roles. Further, the confessions of others define the protagonist. Both Miss Lonelyhearts and Raskolnikov are, as I have said, silent; they are only intermittently articulate and only intermittently conscious. Yet they are both complex. Neither speech nor introspection would, therefore, adequately reveal their preoccupations. The confessions they hear often do reveal them—or echo them, or extend them, or give them articulate form.

The spiritual progress of Raskolnikov and Miss Lonelyhearts is also revealed by a series of dreams. Each series culminates in a vision which signals conversion—Raskolnikov's microbe dream and Miss Lonelyhearts' communion with God. And each series begins with a memorable and prophetic vision whose significance lingers throughout the novel. Miss Lonelyhearts' dream of sacrificing the lamb functions—structurally and symbolically—exactly as does Raskolnikov's dream of the beating and slaughter of the mare. Both are flashback dreams, and both are literally plausible; each could be a real memory. In each dream, an idyllic scene shifts suddenly into a horrible spectacle. In each, the death of an animal is preceded by dreadfully prolonged suffering: the drunken peasants beat the mare with whips, clubs, and poles before finishing it off with an ax; Miss Lonelyhearts saws clumsily at the lamb's throat with a broken knife before smashing its head with a rock. Each dream reveals the hero's ambiguous role. Raskolnikov is simultaneously the murderous peasant with his ax, the tortured mare too weak to pull its load, and the anguished but helpless witness of cruelty (his "real" self in the dream); Miss Lonelyhearts is also simultaneously witness, executioner, and victim. And his dream contains, among other things, a synopsis of his destiny: he is "elected priest" in a blasphemous joke which, because of his inability to perform the priestly function, ends in grotesque terror.

In both *Crime and Punishment* and *Miss Lonelyhearts*, the rhythm of obsession dominates the narrative pattern. Miss Lonelyhearts and Raskolnikov alternate between frenzied, often directionless activity and near-catatonic withdrawal. They roam the world of streets, parks, and taverns, or they collapse into feverish stupor in their rooms. Neither action nor withdrawal works. Activity ends in violence or horror, and stupor is destroyed by the urgency of pain. This alternate frenzy and collapse makes very good psychological sense. It is the familiar and contradictory impulse of anyone whose condition is unbearable but unchangeable. It also becomes, in both novels, a metaphoric expression of the paradox which confronts each protagonist: something must be done, but nothing can be done.

And it becomes a good deal more. The psychology of obsession, as Dostoevski used it, involved a variety of technical devices which, when they appeared in *Miss Lonelyhearts*, were assumed to have come from the surrealists. We should remember, however, that the surrealists claimed Dostoevski as a spiritual father,[18] and that Max Ernst's painting of the surrealist fraternity shows Dostoevski in the front row, holding Ernst himself on his lap.[19] The "surrealist" elements in *Miss Lonelyhearts* were largely anticipated in *Crime and Punishment*. In both novels, the technique of distortion is basically realistic—it derives from the psychology of the hero. Obsession governs the experience of the hero, and the experience of the hero governs that reality the reader perceives. When the rhythm of obsession replaces the normal rhythm of time, external scenes and events become bizarre phenomena. The protagonist's consciousness is counterpointed against the normal rhythm; he awakens and rushes from his room, but it is not dawn which greets him. The streets may be sunny and crowded or black and empty. Or he may wander through the city so absorbed in his obsession that he loses all consciousness of his environment. Awareness suddenly returns with all the force of a mystic experience. Because in his last moment of consciousness the sun was high in the sky, the sudden perception that it is setting is a ghastly and unexplained miracle.

Both Raskolnikov and Miss Lonelyhearts respond to external reality as though it were an apparition or a revelation. They superstitiously read it for clues: Raskolnikov feels that some fate led him to overhear the tavern conversation about justified murder; Miss Lonelyhearts takes his cue from the phallic obelisk. They perceive reality as though it were a dream: Raskolnikov moves through a series of apparitional wagons, paint smells, fourth-floor

[18] See, for example, Wallace Fowlie's *Age of Surrealism*, p. 12.
[19] The painting, dated December, 1922, is reproduced in Maurice Nadeau's *Histoire du Surréalisme*, p. 362.

rooms with yellow wallpaper and "chance" meetings; Miss Lonelyhearts is haunted by sea images, blood, nipples, phalli, flowers. In moments of preoccupation, they collide violently with external reality: Raskolnikov wanders in front of a wagon and is lashed by the coachman; Miss Lonelyhearts, dreaming of children dancing, steps back from the bar, collides with a man, and is punched in the mouth. At other moments, external reality seems only a mirror of the self's preoccupations: after learning of his sister's pursuit by Svidrigailov, Raskolnikov sees in the street a drunken girl pursued by a seducer; when Miss Lonelyhearts decides to call Mrs. Doyle, he finds the walls of the booth covered with obscene drawings. In both cases, the expressive use of external scene or incident is ambiguously meaningful. Raskolnikov's perception of the drunken girl and her pursuer reveals his own obsession, but it also reveals that the predatory evil which obsesses him actually exists. When Miss Lonelyhearts fixes "his eyes on two disembodied genitals" (p. 102), he reveals his own attempt to seize upon sexuality, but he also reveals that the world shares his obsession. And the crudely drawn, disembodied genitals further reveal that debasement of sexuality which makes it powerless to help.

Fantasy, hallucination, and dream are as natural to an obsessive character as theatrical speech is to a self-conscious character. The obsession projects itself outward, and expressionism is then a fact of perception, not just a literary technique. And there are, in the real world, obsessive environments as well as obsessive individuals. The worlds in which Raskolnikov and Miss Lonelyhearts live relentlessly confirm their obsessions. Misery and grotesque deformation are everywhere—outside the self as well as within. As

James said, "The lunatic's visions of horror are all drawn from the material of daily fact." This union of personal obsession and universal reality creates the peculiar stifling atmosphere of both *Crime and Punishment* and *Miss Lonelyhearts*. Life seems to be an airless room or an oppressive dream from which one cannot wake. Appropriately, Svidrigailov remarks that what all men need is fresh air, and Shrike rehearses in parody the various forms of escape.

The psychology of obsession allows Dostoevski to treat his background symbolically without sacrificing the sense of reality. It also allows him to focus relentlessly upon his central themes. Obsession automatically produces unity of action—it perceives only that which is somehow relevant to the obsession. Life becomes, to the obsessive character, a drama in which everything—his surroundings, his actions, his dreams—are symbolic expressions of his own compulsion. When that compulsion derives from an accurate, if partial, vision of life, we have simultaneously the material for problem drama, realistic psychology, and symbolic tragedy. And all of these can be made to produce, as they do in *Crime and Punishment* and *Miss Lonelyhearts*, a unity of effect comparable to that of brilliantly staged drama.

Theatrical comparisons are inevitable. I have already mentioned the stage speech which both West and Dostoevski used, and it is also true that both were fond of stage entrances, exits, and curtain scenes. One could even find in *Hamlet*—or at least in some readings of *Hamlet*—a theatrical ancestor for the psychology and techniques I have described. In both West and Dostoevski, the basically "realistic" stage techniques frequently shade off into deliberate fantasy or contrivance. That Raskolnikov's aimless

wanderings should lead him to the tavern where Svidrigailov waits is a psychologically plausible coincidence; that
Svidrigailov should happen to take rooms next to Sonia
or that Lebeziatnikoff should happen to room with the
Marmeladovs is not. Nor is the erectile shadow of the
obelisk in *Miss Lonelyhearts* literally plausible. Yet, instead
of destroying the sense of reality, these artifices merely
twist it. Both Raskolnikov and Miss Lonelyhearts are aware
of the too appropriate incidents in their dramas. They
struggle against the sense of being actors in a humiliating
charade, of being trapped in a fantasy or a farce.

The number of parallels is nearly inexhaustible. The ambiguous sexuality of the "womanish" Porfiry Petrovitch is
echoed by the Clean Old Man. Lizavetta "looks like a sol-
dier," and Mrs. Doyle looks "like a police captain" (p.
105). Even the basic metaphors of *Miss Lonelyhearts* can
be found in *Crime and Punishment*. Miss Lonelyhearts is
"like a dead man" (p. 79) himself, and he broods upon the
"dead world" and the necessity of "bringing it to life" (p.
39). Raskolnikov is fascinated by the story of Lazarus.
That parable of resurrection becomes, in *Crime and Punishment*, an insistent analogue to Raskolnikov's own deadness
and ultimate rebirth. The prevailing deadness in both novels is echoed by Shrike, with his "dead pan," and by Svidrigailov, with his irritable ennui and ultimate suicide. The
metaphor of death and resurrection is, of course, fundamental to Christianity. Its use by two different authors is
hardly startling. But neither, in this case, is it coincidental.
West, I think, deliberately borrowed and inverted the
terms of Dostoevski's contrast between life and death.
Throughout *Crime and Punishment*, theory is opposed to
life—life is organic, creative, concrete, infinite while theory

is mechanical, dead, abstract, finite. Raskolnikov is reborn when he abandons his theory and submits to the diversity and uncertainty of life. But in *Miss Lonelyhearts,* the diversity of life is what destroys. The sea of life spawns nothing but junk—proliferating debris incapable of meaningful unity. Even in fantasy, Miss Lonelyhearts is overwhelmed by "marine refuse" (p. 116). His contacts with the nature-worshipping Betty and that embodiment of the life force, Mrs. Doyle, unite to destroy him—it is his affair with Mrs. Doyle that sends Doyle after him, and it is the pregnant Betty who cuts off Doyle's escape and makes the grotesque accident of Miss Lonelyhearts' death inevitable. In *Miss Lonelyhearts,* the life force is, like the sexuality of *Balso Snell,* governed by the "mechanics of decay."

It should be clear that West did not just prune away words with his pair of shears. He snipped off *Crime and Punishment*'s affirmative epilogue entirely, and he diminished more than the physical bulk of the rest of the novel. Scenes, speeches, characters have all drastically shrunk. Betty is a trivial Sonia, and Shrike is, compared to Svidrigailov, a stunted dwarf. Even the artificial conventions of *Crime and Punishment* have been made far more formal —the vast stage has become a puppet theater whose sets are obviously painted and abruptly changed, whose scenes move with the jerky animation of a cartoon, whose plot is as relentless as a syllogism. Obviously, there is a corresponding diminution of both dramatic power and psychological complexity. We need not argue that West was Dostoevski's equal. But we need not rank him among Dostoevski's imitators either. Miss Lonelyhearts' whole career implicitly repudiates the "solution" of *Crime and Punishment.* It takes Dostoveskian premises and makes them yield a conclusion which denies Dostoevskian answers, even parodying, in the person of Betty, Dostoevski's favorite instrument of salvation—the naïve representative of orthodox faith and instinctive love. And West did not just reproduce the techniques he took from Dostoevski. He exploited their possibilities in ways Dostoevski did not, and he deftly united them with apparently unrelated techniques borrowed from a variety of other writers and other arts. Though his borrowings from *Crime and Punishment* were in part respectful, they were hardly slavish. The case history of Raskolnikov merges, in West's hands, with other familiar histories to produce a truly classic case.

Gleanings from Antic Hay

I was a ridiculous actor of heroic parts who deserved to be laughed at—and *was* laughed at. But then every man is ludicrous if you look at him from outside, without taking into account what's going on in his heart and mind. You could turn Hamlet into an epigrammatic farce with an inimitable scene when he takes his adored mother in adultery. You could make the wittiest Guy de Maupassant short story out of the life of Christ, by contrasting the mad rabbi's pretensions with his abject fate. . . . Every one's a walking farce and a walking tragedy at the same time. The man who slips on a banana-skin and fractures his skull describes against the sky, as he falls, the most richly comical arabesque.—Lypiatt, in *Antic Hay*.[20]

If *Crime and Punishment* is (except for the Epilogue) a tragedy played against the constant threat of incipient farce, *Antic Hay* is a farce played against the flickering sense of real pain and real loss. Lypiatt's remarks about comedy are obviously appropriate to *Miss Lonelyhearts*. So

[20] *Antic Hay*, p. 208.

are several other aspects of *Antic Hay*. The early Huxley
was, like West, fascinated by banal self-dramatization
(Lypiatt's heroic posturing and Rosie Shearwater's great-
lady poses) and by self-conscious adoption of theatrical
masks (Gumbril's padded coat and false beard, Coleman's
satanism). As I have already remarked,[21] Coleman is a direct
ancestor of Shrike. He is a mocking intellectual and seducer
who preaches the delights of sin in a language composed of
blasphemous doggerel, church Latin, vulgarisms, and stage
rhetoric. Like Shrike, his gestures are mechanically frenzied. He is forever shouting, thumping the floor with his
stick, and laughing "his ferocious, artificial laugh." His eyes
sparkle "blue fire, like an electric machine." His mock
exclamations, his blasphemies, his fake ecstasies and angers
are all remarkably like Shrike's. When he is asked why he
adopted a beard,

> "For religious reasons," he said and made the sign of the
> cross.
> > "Christ-like in my behaviour,
> > Like every good believer,
> > I imitate the Saviour
> > And cultivate a beaver."

[21] See Chapter II, which discusses the minor traces of *Antic Hay*
visible in *Balso Snell*. I may as well record here some minor traces
visible in *Miss Lonelyhearts*. At one point, Gumbril muses about all the
legless beggars and phthisical charwomen whose misery lurks on the
periphery of civilized life, and he is also distressed to find copper
coins "trespassing" among the silver in his right-hand pocket. "Silver
was for the right hand, copper for the left. It was one of the laws. . . ."
Miss Lonelyhearts says that man's tropism for order means "Keys in
one pocket, change in another. . . . [But] keys yearn to mix with
change" (pp. 115–16). For the original suggestion that *Antic Hay* is
relevant to West, I am indebted to William Peden's review of West's
Collected Works. Peden remarks, in passing, that Shrike is a "blood-
brother to the Satanic Coleman of Huxley's 'Antic Hay.' " Peden,
"Nathanael West."

Shrike's first appearance (in the speakeasy) follows almost exactly the pattern of Coleman's first appearance (in a restaurant).

"The kidneys!" In an ecstasy of delight, Coleman thumped the floor with the ferrule of his stick. "The kidneys! Tell me all about kidneys.". . . Coleman clapped his hands. "The key," he cried, "the key. Out of the trouser pocket of babes and sucklings it comes. The genuine, the unique Yale. How right I was to come here to-night! But, holy Sephiroth, there's my trollop."

He picked up his stick. . . . A woman was standing near the door. Coleman came up to her, pointed without speaking to the table, and returned, driving her along in front of him, tapping her gently over the haunches with his stick, as one might drive a docile animal to the slaughter.

"Allow me to introduce," said Coleman, "the sharer of my joys and sorrows. *La compagne de mes nuits blanches et de mes jours plutôt sales.* In a word, Zoe."²²

"To the renaissance!" [Shrike] kept shouting. "To the renaissance! To the brown Greek manuscripts and mistresses with the great smooth marbly limbs. . . . but that reminds me, I'm expecting one of my admirers—a coweyed girl of great intelligence." He illustrated the word *intelligence* by carving two enormous breasts in the air with his hands. . . .

At this moment . . . the young woman expected by Shrike came up to the bar. . . .

"Miss Farkis," Shrike said, making her bow as a ventriloquist does his doll, "Miss Farkis, I want you to meet Miss Lonelyhearts.". . .

"Miss Farkis," Shrike said, "Miss Farkis works in a book store and writes on the side." He patted her rump. (Pp. 27–29.)

²² Huxley, pp. 45–47.

Despite some additional similarities, West's debt to Huxley is far smaller than his debt to Dostoevski. It consists chiefly in Coleman's mannerisms and rhetoric, both of which West improved. As usual, he condensed and polished his borrowed material and then gave it a meaningful twist. Coleman is, despite his mannerisms and poses, physically impressive—he is called a Cossack by one character—but Shrike is a puppet whose features "huddled together in a dead, gray triangle" beneath the "shining white globe of his brow" (p. 27). The contrast between his orgiastic rhetoric and his puny deadness is both more comic and more sinister than Coleman's theatrical satanism. And Shrike's bullying becomes, for the same reason, far more vicious than Coleman's bluster.

Prose Poems, Hallucinations, Dreams

[Man] has sought . . . in all climates and in all times, some means of escaping, were it only for a few hours, from his home in the mire. . . .[23]—Baudelaire.

Or, as Miss Lonelyhearts says, "Men have always fought their misery with dreams" (p. 146). The influence of the symbolist poets upon West is as generally acknowledged as the influence of Dostoevski. It too was noted by Angel Flores in 1933, and it too has been expounded several times since, notably by Marc L. Ratner.[24] Flores quite properly

---

[23] *Les Paradis Artificiels* in *Prose and Poetry*, trans. Arthur Symons, p. 238.

[24] Ratner, "Anywhere out of This World: Baudelaire and Nathanael West," pp. 456–63. Ratner's article combines an essentially sound discussion of the influence of symbolist prose poems on West with an interpretation of *Miss Lonelyhearts* which seems to me seriously mistaken. Ratner appears to miss the irony in both Miss Lonelyhearts' affair with Betty and his final "communion" with God.

expanded the symbolist influence into a tradition which runs from Coleridge to the surrealists, and he concluded that "West's most remarkable performance has been to bring Fyodor's dark angels into the Haunted Castle. . . ."[25] This remark seems to me both astute and misleading. West certainly did fuse symbolist techniques with Dostoevskian themes, but that fusion was not as remarkable as Flores seems to suggest. For one thing, Fyodor's dark angels were first brought into the Haunted Castle by Dostoevski himself, not by West. As I have already argued, *Crime and Punishment* is an hallucinatory, symbolic novel. And Dostoevski touches Baudelaire at so many points that West's fusion of the two was more inevitable than remarkable. Both Baudelaire and Dostoevski repeatedly analyze the evils of egoism, the voluptuous pleasure of remorse, the stupidity of liberal utopianism, and the sin of ennui with its consequent spite and spiritual deadness. Like Dostoevski, Baudelaire is fond of treating the imprisoned self and its fantasies of escape. "Life is a hospital in which every patient is possessed by the desire to change his bed. . . ."[26] The narrator of "Anywhere out of the World" considers going to Lisbon, Holland, Batavia, Tornio, the Baltic, the Pole, until: "At last my soul bursts into speech, and wisely cries to me: Anywhere, anywhere, as long as it be out of this world!"[27] Ratner has suggested that this rehearsal of escapes was the model for Shrike's parodies on the South Seas, art, hedonism, and return to the soil.[28] It may well have been. I would add, however, that Svidrigailov indulges

---

[25] Flores, p. 1.
[26] Baudelaire, *Petits Poèmes en Prose* in *Prose and Poetry*, pp. 80–81.
[27] *Ibid.*
[28] Ratner, p. 458.

in a similar rehearsal. He tells Raskolnikov that he may get married, or he may go to America, or he may go up in a balloon, or he may go on a journey where he will not need money. The last alternative, a disguised reference to suicide, is the one he adopts and the one which literally takes him out of this world.

Baudelaire's description of the "artificial paradise" of hashish intoxication is directly relevant to *Miss Lonelyhearts*. It is, like Miss Lonelyhearts' career, a paradigm of the progress of delusion. To Baudelaire, the intoxication was evil not just because it was false but because it parodied religious experience. It carried the romantic egoist to damnation, not redemption. This is his description of the typical victim:

> A temperament half nervous and half splenetic seems to me to be the most favourable for the development of this particular intoxication; to this I shall add a cultivated mind, given to the study of form and colour; a tender heart, made weary by unhappiness, but still youthful; if you will allow me, I shall go so far as to endow him with past faults, and, what must be the natural result in a nature easily aroused, if not positive remorse, at least a regret for time ill-spent and profaned. A taste for metaphysics, a knowledge of the different philosophical hypotheses regarding human destiny, are certainly not useless attributes, as are, no less, a love for virtue, for abstract, stoic, or mystical virtue, which is to be found in all books on which the modern child is fed, and which is declared to be the highest summit to which a distinguished spirit might attain. If I add to all this a delicate sensibility, that I omitted as a superogatory condition, I believe that I shall have gathered together the general elements commonly attributed to the modern man with a sensitive nature. . . . Let us now see what will become of this individual driven to

distraction by Haschisch. Let us follow the development of his imagination to its ultimate and most splendid resting-place, to the man's belief in his own Divinity. . . . there develops that mysterious and temporary state of the spirit, when the full depth of life, beset with multiple problems, completely reveals itself in the spectacle before one's eyes, be that spectacle natural or merely trivial—when the first object seen becomes the perfect symbol. . . .

A strange good-will manifested even toward strangers, a kind of philanthropy that owes more to pity than to love (here appears the first germ of that satanic spirit which will develop later in an extraordinary fashion) but which goes so far as to fear hurting anyone. . . . Cult, Adoration, Prayer, dreams of happiness surge and dart forth with the fierce energy and brilliance of fireworks. . . .

He confounds completely dream with action, and his imagination becoming more and more enthusiastic before the enchanting spectacle of his corrected and idealized nature, substituting this fascinating picture of himself for his real individuality, so weak in will, so rich in vanity. . . .

No one should be astonished at the final, the supreme thought born in the dreamer's mind: *I have become God!*[29]

There are obvious differences, as well as similarities, between this hypothetical case history and Miss Lonelyhearts' experience. For one thing, Miss Lonelyhearts' delusion is achieved without drugs. Baudelaire, however, speaks of "each man's natural dose of opium"[30] and consistently describes drugs as collaborators with, not just agents acting upon, an individual's natural tendencies. And the psycho-

[29] Baudelaire, *Les Paradis* . . . , pp. 267–68, 271–72, 274–75.
[30] Baudelaire, *Petits Poèmes* . . . , p. 28.

logical stages through which the dreamer passes correspond closely to Miss Lonelyhearts' pattern.

More important, the symbolist techniques were perfectly suited to West's rewriting Dostoevski with a pair of shears. In *Crime and Punishment*, psychological states tend to be acted out, not just revealed. Symbolic background is often panoramic, not focused in a single detail. West reduced symbolic actions to isolated gestures and symbolic scenes to single images. Miss Lonelyhearts is repeatedly in that state "when the first object seen becomes the perfect symbol"—a phallic obelisk, a poster in a bar, a newspaper struggling in an empty sky. Further, the symbolist prose poem naturally fuses with the Dostoevskian set speech. Both are essentially essays, expositions of a psychological state or a meaningful experience or an abstract idea. By combining the two forms, West united the epigrammatic terseness and the suggestive imagery of the symbolists with the dramatic and narrative relevance of the set speech. Shrike's speeches, for example, are highly polished prose poems. They are also expressions of character, influences upon Miss Lonelyhearts' destiny, and significant comments within the philosophical context of the novel.

The difficulty with the Baudelairean prose poem is that it tends to be entirely too lucid and self-contained. When dropped into a narrative, it may be a lump which refuses to blend. West solved this difficulty in part by also borrowing the kaleidoscopic techniques of Rimbaud. His prose often echoes Rimbaudian rhythms.

[*A Season in Hell*]: A villein, I must have made the journey to the Holy Land. . . . A leper, I am seated among potsherds and nettles, at the foot of a sun-eaten wall.—Later, a reiter, I must have bivouacked under German stars.[31]

[*Miss Lonelyhearts*]: Without dreaming he was aware of fireflies and the slop of oceans. Later a train rolled into a station where he was a reclining statue holding a stopped clock, a coach rumbled into the yard of an inn where he was sitting over a guitar, cap in hand, shedding the rain with his hump. (P. 188.)

Rimbaud's shifting and dissolving images are as perfectly suited to transitional states of consciousness as the Baudelairean prose poem is to a single vision or idea.

Once again, West also borrowed from, and parodied, Huysmans. Shrike's description of the hedonist's last party is a radically compressed parody of a similar dinner in *Against the Grain:*

[Huysmans]: The dining-room was hung with black and looked out on a strangely metamorphosed garden, the walks being strewn with charcoal, the little basin in the middle of the lawn bordered with a rim of black basalt and filled with ink; and the ordinary shrubs superseded by cypresses and pines. The dinner itself was served on a black cloth . . . illuminated by candelabra in which tall tapers flared.

While a concealed orchestra played funeral marches, the guests were waited on by naked negresses. . . .

The viands were served on black-bordered plates,—turtle soup, Russian black bread, ripe olives from Turkey, caviar . . . game dished up in sauces colored to resemble liquorice water and boot-blacking. . . .[32]

---

[31] Arthur Rimbaud, *A Season in Hell and The Drunken Boat*, trans. Louise Varèse, p. 9.
[32] Huysmans, *Against the Grain*, p. 89.

[Shrike]: "The guests are dressed in black, the waiters are coons, the table is a coffin carved for you by Eric Gill. You serve caviar and blackberries and liquorice candy and coffee without cream." (P. 125.)

Huysmans characteristically used a "surrealist" device—describing natural scenes as though they were artificial—which West borrowed, though he changed its flavor.

[Huysmans]: The plain lay partly in the shadows cast by the hills, while the centre, where the moonlight fell, looked as if it were powdered with starch and smeared with cold-cream. . . .[33]

[West]: The gray sky looked as if it had been rubbed with a soiled eraser (p. 25).

And Huysmans also used the corollary to this device—endowing inanimate objects with life. West's phallic obelisk with its rapidly lengthening shadow was anticipated by the various scenes in which Huysmans described church pillars and forests in deliberately phallic imagery.

Huysmans' literary theories are also pertinent to *Miss Lonelyhearts*. His hero, Des Esseintes, regarded the prose poem as the ideal form—with Baudelaire and Mallarmé as its masters—and worried about how to transfer it to the novel.

Again and again Des Esseintes had pondered the distracting problem, how to write a novel concentrated in a few sentences, but which should yet contain the cohobated juice of the hundreds of pages always taken up in describing the setting, sketching the characters, gathering

[33] *Ibid.*, p. 106. Light mentions Huysmans in connection with *Miss Lonelyhearts*, but only as a source for that opposition between flesh and spirit which Light feels is central to West's work. See Light, pp. 91–92.

together the necessary incidental observations and minor details.[34]

Huysmans himself never solved the problem. His novels are prolix, often dull, sometimes unintentionally ludicrous, and almost totally static. His novelistic prose poems sacrifice the compression of Baudelaire and Mallarmé without gaining dramatic unity or narrative continuity. And his prose is so flavored with artificial spices that "decadent" seems the only accurate critical term. He is, I think, convincing only when he describes the aberrations of lust and his own fascinated revulsion from everything female. Yet he was oddly useful to West. His style, in West's hands, undergoes a variety of parodies, from the direct ridicule of *Balso Snell* to the compressed borrowings of *Miss Lonelyhearts* to the curious new applications we shall examine in *A Cool Million* and *The Day of the Locust*. And of course West made the ideal of "a novel concentrated in a few sentences" his own.

> Lyric novels can be written according to Poe's definition of a lyric poem. . . .
> Leave slow growth to the book reviewers, you only have time to explode. Remember William Carlos William's description of the pioneer women who shot their children against the wilderness like cannonballs. Do the same with your novels.[35]

West's reference to Poe merely cites, of course, the classic source for symbolist theories about the short poem and unity of effect. Baudelaire repeated Poe's theories and added the injunction: "Be always a poet, even in prose."[36]

---

[34] Huysmans, *Against the Grain*, pp. 324–25.

[35] West, "Some Notes on Miss Lonelyhearts," p. 2.

[36] Baudelaire, "My Heart Laid Bare," quoted in Pascal Pia, *Baudelaire*, trans. Patrick Gregory, p. 106.

Huysmans transferred the ideal from poems and tales to the novel, and West, in *Miss Lonelyhearts*, actually wrote a novel which meets the symbolist criteria.

But West took from the symbolists more than his reliance on hallucinatory images and the ideal of a poetic, highly compressed prose. The typical symbolist hero was perhaps as important to him as any symbolist techniques. From Poe to Huysmans, the dandy reigns supreme. He is always morbidly sensitive, exacerbated by vulgarity, tormented by dreams and fantasies, weak-willed but compulsive, fond of attenuated emotions and aesthetic eccentricities, perverse, disintegrating, withdrawn. This description would, I think, apply equally to Roderick Usher and to Des Esseintes. It would also apply in many ways to Miss Lonelyhearts, except that West's treatment of the symbolist character implicitly repudiates the symbolist values. Edmund Wilson has observed that the symbolist hero usually dwells in a state of neurotic isolation, "encouraging [his] private manias, ultimately preferring [his] absurdest chimeras to the most astonishing contemporary realities, ultimately mistaking [his] chimeras for realities."[37] Even when dandyism is mixed with religion—as it is in Huysmans—the focus remains relentlessly on the self. The dramatic issue is the self's damnation or redemption, and the way of Grace leads not into the world but into further isolation from it—Axel's castle is simply exchanged for the cloister. The Christianity of the symbolists is, therefore, often as decadent as their dandyism. Neurotic isolation is a badge of superiority. The people, not the devil, symbolize all that is evil; and vulgarity,

[37] Edmund Wilson, *Axel's Castle: A Study in the Imaginative Literature of 1870–1930*, p. 287.

not pride or concupiscence, is the taint of the Beast. West, however, was not much interested in the superiorities of the sensitive soul. He took the common symbolist materials —a neurotic, exacerbated hero in a vulgarized world —and drew from them his own conclusion: in the vulgarization of modern life, it is the masses who are the real victims. "Men have always fought their misery with dreams. Although dreams were once powerful, they have been made puerile by the movies, radio and newspapers. Among many betrayals, this one is the worst." (P. 146.) The fact of sordid misery compels Miss Lonelyhearts' quest. Though he is "sick" himself, there is no escape for him in personal salvation. He must redeem the suffering of others to fulfill his mission, and his final delusion and death are a failure, not a martyrdom—he becomes just another victim of a world he could not change and could not escape except by ceasing to exist.

The burden of *Miss Lonelyhearts* is finally, therefore, far more Dostoevskian than symbolist. Its hero attempts significant action in a context of other lives whose fate is entangled with his own—lives which may even be more important that his own. And the emphasis upon mass suffering was only one of West's departures from the symbolists. Where Baudelaire contrasted the "artificial paradise" of hashish intoxication with religious experience, West made them equivalent. In the world of *Miss Lonelyhearts*, all paradise is artificial. The religious faith which furnished Baudelaire and Huysmans a way out of this world becomes, in West, just another pipe dream, as fatal as it is false.

Psychology and the Waste Land

Psychology has nothing to do with reality nor should it be used as motivation. The novelist is no longer a psycholo-

gist. Psychology can become something much more important. The great body of case histories can be used in
the way the ancient writers used their myths. Freud is
your Bulfinch; you can not learn from him.—West, "Some
Notes on Miss Lonelyhearts."[38]

Though they may be unnecessarily epigrammatic, these
remarks clearly repudiate psychology—any psychology—
as a system of revealed truth. It is therefore interesting that
two of the three long studies on West which have appeared
should expound psychoanalytic readings of *Miss Lonelyhearts*.[39] It is even more interesting—or odd—that West's
comments should be cited to support them, but that is
exactly what has happened. Here, for example, is the way
Victor Comerchero has construed West's remarks: "Freud
(psychoanalysis) has delved so deeply into the human
psyche that the analytic novel has been rendered sterile.
'The novelist is no longer a psychologist,' because the
novelist can offer no new psychological insights."[40] Following Stanley Edgar Hyman, Comerchero then asserts that
Miss Lonelyhearts embodies, in orthodox Freudian terms,
an Oedipal case history of repressed homosexuality, and he
concludes with this description of Miss Lonelyhearts' religious experience:

> What Miss Lonelyhearts *really* accepts is his castration.
> The religious conversion is *really* a conversion from latent
> to overt homosexuality; so is the ending. The final em-
> brace between Miss Lonelyhearts and Doyle is, as Stanley
> Edgar Hyman has noted, "a homosexual tableau—the men

[38] West, "Some Notes on Miss Lonelyhearts," p. 2.
[39] Hyman, pp. 22–24, and Comerchero, pp. 84 and 95–100.
[40] Comerchero, p. 95. Hyman quotes West's remarks but does not
attempt to construe them. Unlike Comerchero, however, he seems aware
that they do not support a Freudian reading. Hyman, p. 24.

locked in embrace while the woman stands helplessly by."[41]

The emphasis upon the "really's" is mine. I supply it for two reasons: to underscore Comerchero's flat contradiction of West's own statement ("Psychology has nothing to do with reality")[42] and to underscore the assumption behind too many exercises in "Freudian" literary criticism—that Freudian theory is not just an interpretative method but reality itself. Whatever the merits of such an assumption, West did not share it. His remarks indicate that we should regard Freud the way modern intellectuals regard classic fables, not the way devout believers regard their scriptures.

West's remarks do not, of course, prove that Freudian interpretation is irrelevant to *Miss Lonelyhearts*. The test of any interpretation is its ability to illuminate a text, not its endorsement by the author. But we need not invoke West's authority to demonstrate that the Hyman-Comerchero reading fails even that fundamental test. Hyman offers this hypothetical case history for Miss Lonelyhearts:

> Terrified of his stern religious father, identifying with his soft loving mother, the boy renounces his phallicism out of castration anxiety—a classic Oedipus complex. In these terms the Shrikes are Miss Lonelyhearts' Oedipal parents, abstracted as the father's loud voice and the mother's tantalizing breast. The scene at the end of Miss Lonelyhearts' date with Mary Shrike is horrifying and superb. Standing outside her apartment door, suddenly overcome with passion, he strips her naked under her fur coat while

[41] Comerchero, pp. 99–100.

[42] Comerchero is not alone in this contradiction. Even Daniel Aaron, normally a reliable critic, left the "not" out of West's "Freud" sentence when quoting it, and thus neatly turned West's meaning on its head. See Aaron, "Late Thoughts on Nathanael West," p. 310.

she keeps talking mindlessly of her mother's death, mumbling and repeating herself, so that Shrike will not hear their sudden silence and come out. Finally Mary agrees to let Miss Lonelyhearts in if Shrike is not home, goes inside, and soon Shrike peers out the door, wearing only the top of his pajamas. It is the child's Oedipal vision perfectly dramatized: he can clutch at his mother's body but loses her each time to his more potent rival.[43]

This sounds plausible enough, but it contains a disconcerting number of inventions, misstatements, and omissions. From the novel, we know only that Miss Lonelyhearts' father was a minister, not that he was stern or loud-voiced or that Miss Lonelyhearts was terrified of him. The only evidence that Miss Lonelyhearts even had a mother—hard or soft, loving or cruel—is the fact of his own existence. Further, Miss Lonelyhearts is not "suddenly overcome with passion." Instead, he is trying "to work this spark [of desire] into a flame," (p. 91) trying "desperately to keep the spark alive" (p. 92). Mary is so far from being the object—maternal or otherwise—of his desire that his sexual response is an effort of the will, not a passionate act. Her "tantalizing breast" fails to tantalize. And the case history ignores the connivance of the Shrikes in the comedy enacted, a comedy in which Miss Lonelyhearts is perhaps the most passive and innocent party. The comedy's chief author is, of course, Shrike himself. Mary tells Miss Lonelyhearts that Shrike lets her go out with other men because "He knows that I let them neck me and when I get home all hot and bothered, why he climbs into my bed and begs for

[43] Hyman, pp. 23–24. Hyman observes—accurately—that "if this is the pattern of Miss Lonelyhearts' Oedipus complex, it is not that of West, nor are the Shrikes the pattern of West's parents" (p. 24). Comerchero quotes Hyman's "case history" with approval. See Comerchero, p. 84.

it" (p. 85). In the hallway she says: "We can't stop talking.
We must talk. Willie probably heard the elevator and is
listening behind the door. You don't know him. If he
doesn't hear us talk, he'll know you're kissing me and open
the door. It's an old trick of his." (Pp. 91–92.) It is indeed.
And if we want to identify latent homosexuals, I suggest
that Shrike is a far more obvious suspect than Miss Lonelyhearts.

Hyman's interpretation requires him to read the novel's
ending as a revelation of repressed desire.

> It is of course a homosexual tableau—the men locked in
> embrace while the woman stands helplessly by. . . .
> It is West's ultimate irony that the symbolic embrace
> they manage at the end is one penetrating the body of the
> other with a bullet.[44]

Again, this is persuasive until one reads the novel. The
embrace is "symbolic" enough, but it is hardly suggestive
of homosexuality. Doyle shouts a warning, but Miss Lonelyhearts "did not understand the cripple's shout and heard
it as a cry for help from Desperate, Harold S., Catholic-
mother, Broken-hearted, Broad-shoulders, Sick-of-it-all,
Disillusioned-with-tubercular-husband. He was running to
succor them with love." (P. 212.) Miss Lonelyhearts has
clearly lost all sense of particular identity. The object of his
embrace has neither sex nor substance. It is an abstraction, a
compound illusion projected upon a real person whom Miss
Lonelyhearts barely recognizes. And Doyle, the other
party to the "homosexual tableau," tries to escape the embrace and also tries to get rid of the gun. It is the entry of

---

[44] Hyman, pp. 22–23.

the "helpless" Betty, "cutting off his escape," which leads to the grotesque accident of Miss Lonelyhearts' death.

The homosexual interpretation is, then, so weak that it requires us to ignore many of the novel's details and invent others. It is also quite irrelevant to the novel's issues. Nothing in the diagnosis explains the fact of mass suffering or the reasons for Miss Lonelyhearts' response to that suffering or the ultimate failure of his mission. Heterosexuality is no doubt desirable, but it is hardly sufficient to permit the successful imitation of Christ, and in the world of Miss Lonelyhearts nothing less than the imitation of Christ can really help.[45] To read the novel as a case of repressed homosexuality is to read it as though Betty had written it. The clinical attitude mimics Betty's blindness to evil and her insistence upon regarding Miss Lonelyhearts as an isolated specimen of morbid illness, not as a man responding intelligibly to a real external situation. "No morality, only medicine." Significantly, Hyman becomes tone deaf to irony whenever Betty appears. He speaks of Betty's "Edenic innocence," of her "patient innocence . . . that makes the book so heartbreaking," and concludes that "she represents . . . the innocent order of Nature, as opposed to the disorder of sinful Man."[46] This is nonsense. It is the "innocent

---

[45] Significantly, neither Hyman nor Comerchero is able to relate the homosexual interpretation to any important aspect of the novel. Its essential irrelevance can easily be demonstrated. For example: let us assume that "latent homosexuality" is an accurate diagnosis, and let us assume that Miss Lonelyhearts is either "cured" of his repressed tendencies or brought to accept them. He could then marry Betty and go into advertising or marry Doyle and go into interior decorating. What effect would either resolution have? None at all. Hyman and Comerchero do not, of course, pretend that homosexuality is Miss Lonelyhearts' only problem, but I do not think they have demonstrated that it is, in terms of the novel's major themes, any kind of problem at all.

[46] Hyman, pp. 27 and 17.

order of Nature," of course, which produces the cruel disorder of a girl born with no nose, an idiot child, an unwanted pregnancy. And Betty's innocence is hardly Eve-like. Though she means well and deserves some sympathy, she is unintelligent and even somewhat corrupt. Her "patient innocence" ignores not only mass suffering but the meaning of this suffering to Miss Lonelyhearts, and her devotion to him is therefore not impressive. And her formula for successful living—country idylls supported by a job in advertising—does not strike me as Edenic.[47]

West's own remarks on psychology are interesting apart from the question of clinical interpretation. We should note initially that he did not introduce his notes as the credo of a lifetime, but as "some of the things I thought when writing [*Miss Lonelyhearts*]." We have no right, therefore, to assume that they were more than working principles for a single book. Yet those working principles are important. "Psychology has nothing to do with reality nor should it be used as motivation." This statement implies an absolute distinction between reality and psychological interpretations of it. It explicitly denies that any psychological theory reveals the "real" motives for behavior. "The novelist is no longer a psychologist"—no longer, that is, a fabricator and explainer of motives. "Psychology can become something much more important. The great body of case histories can be used in the way the ancient writers used their myths." How did the ancient writers use their myths? As established stories whose plausibility did not have to be justi-

---

[47] Hyman, however, is so infatuated with Betty, that he offers repressed homosexuality to "explain" Miss Lonelyhearts' discontent with her (p. 23). Betty's triviality and incomprehension are surely sufficient explanations in themselves.

fied. Sophocles, for example, does not have to convince his audience that the murder of Laius and the marriage of Oedipus and Jocasta are plausible. Both events have the status of facts for which Sophocles does not have to account—not, at least, in the way that George Eliot has to account for the marriage of Dorothea and Causabon. Further, he need not laboriously explain what happened because the audience already knows what happened—the writer can focus on the critical issues in his story without having to document it or rationalize it. The resulting gain in economy is obvious. In one sense, therefore, West's remarks on psychology are only a particular application of his general theory of the lyric novel. West wanted to relieve the novel of its burden of documentation, and the use of familiar materials was fundamental to this aim. "The novelist is no longer a psychologist" in the sense that he no longer has to contrive and heavily document his own case histories; instead, he can borrow his stories from sources which are as familiar to modern readers as myths were to the ancients. But the case history is all he should borrow. "Freud is your Bulfinch; you can not learn from him"—a remark which reduces Freud to the status of an anthologist. We could paraphrase it as "take the data and let the interpretations go." West's attitude may be extreme but it is also extremely clear: Freudian theory can teach you nothing about reality. Freudian case histories, however, like any collection of familiar stories, can be both useful and important to a writer. And West implies that a writer should exercise the same freedom in his use of borrowed case histories that Euripides did in his use of traditional myths.[48]

⁴⁸ I suspect that West's attitude is deliberately overstated. His consistent practice is to accept usable material from any source but to insist

West's use of psychology relies, however, on more than the familiarity of particular materials. He said that Miss Lonelyhearts' "case is classical and is built on all the cases in James' *Varieties of Religious Experience* and Starbuck's *Psychology of Religion*," and I have argued that it is built on other case histories—notably Raskolnikov's—as well. The generic quality of this method is crucial. A classical case history is a type; it is formed by abstracting the common features from many histories until a pattern emerges, a pattern which will be familiar even if the particular materials from which it is formed are not. And the pattern is likely to be persuasive apart from its familiarity. The logic of character becomes, in West's hands, almost musical. It rests upon the internal rhythm and harmony of a sequence of behavior, not upon assignable motives taken from depth psychology or from "rational" theories about human personality. "Psychologizing" can therefore be cut out of the novel. A "classical" pattern of behavior does not need to be explained to be believed; its ubiquity is ample proof of its plausibility.

But what of its meaning? The question is treacherous. It cannot be answered by any psychological analysis which ignores the novel's principal themes. Take, for example, that sexual deadness in Miss Lonelyhearts which both

---

upon evaluating that material himself. In this sense, his attitude toward Freud is not necessarily different from his attitude toward Dostoevski. West asserts in part that the writer himself must ultimately judge the nature of reality, not accept a definition of it from Freud or any other source. This distinction should be kept in mind in considering his own work. The clinical attitude often implies that philosophical or religious beliefs are just rationalizations of individual neuroses, but in *Miss Lonelyhearts* individual neuroses are just particular forms of the prevailing conditions of life.

Hyman and Comerchero regard as presumptive evidence of homosexuality. The deadness is certainly there. Though Mary's excitement is revealed in the changed scent of her body, "no similar change ever took place in his own body, however. Like a dead man, only friction could make him warm or violence make him mobile." (Pp. 78–79.) He tries to "excite himself . . . by thinking of the play Mary made with her breasts. . . . But the excitement refused to come. If anything, he felt colder than before he had started to think of women. It was not his line." (Pp. 79–80.) And when he tries to tease himself with the prospect of Fay Doyle, he remains "as dry and cold as a polished bone" (p. 102).

The evidence is abundant, but what does it mean? If the deadness were limited to Miss Lonelyhearts' sexuality, diagnosis might be simple—but it is not. Deadness pervades all his responses. When he tries to preach the gospel of divine love, he can only produce the mock rhetoric of Shrike, and he feels "like an empty bottle, shiny and sterile" (p. 182). Even his sympathy is deadened by "the stone that had formed in his gut" (p. 25), a stone which, by the novel's end, has become an impervious Gibraltar: "He did not feel guilty. He did not feel. The rock was a solidification of his feeling, his conscience, his sense of reality, his self-knowledge." (P. 206.) And deadness is as pervasive in Miss Lonelyhearts' world as it is in Miss Lonelyhearts himself. The newspapermen in the speakeasy are just "machines for making jokes" (p. 63). Shrike is a master of the "dead pan" whose features "huddled together in a dead, gray triangle" (p. 27), and Mrs. Doyle's massive hams are "like two enormous grindstones" (p. 106). In the park, "the decay that covered the surface of the mottled ground

was not the kind in which life generates" (pp. 23–24).
Even the country idyll has its images of deadness: "In the
deep shade there was nothing but death—rotten leaves,
gray and white fungi, and over everything a funereal hush"
(p. 139).
The world of Miss Lonelyhearts is a waste land.[49] Its
psychology owes far more to regenerative myths than to
Freud and far more to ascetic or apocalyptic Christianity
than to Jessie L. Weston. The world confirms the saint's
anguished vision of this life. It reaches but to dust. Nature
and sexuality are agents of death, alive only in their power
to hurt. Though latent homosexuality is not relevant to the
novel's major themes, universally crippled and malignant
sexuality is. The two representatives of fleshly love—Shrike
and Mrs. Doyle—are described in imagery which is grotesquely symbolic. Shrike's name, for example, comes from
the butcher bird which impales its living prey on thorns,
and the sense of murderous penetration is in his every act.
Mrs. Doyle, however, is omnivorously engulfing. The sexes
are thereby given nightmarish attributes: the phallus is just
an instrument of sadistic impalment, and the female genita-
lia are a smothering, swallowing, devouring sea. Miss Lonelyhearts is quite properly terrified of both sexes. And quite
properly sympathetic to both. Like all the other forces in
the novel, the sexes are, in their active forms, irreconcilable
and mutually destructive. But in their passive forms, both
sexes are victims—Doyle, Mary Shrike, the idiot girl, even
Shrike himself. " 'She's selfish. She's a damned selfish bitch.

[49] The basic waste-land image obviously derives from Eliot. Edmond
L. Volpe has even argued that *Miss Lonelyhearts* is consciously "an
answer to the optimism implicit in Eliot's vision of man and society."
See Volpe, "The Waste Land of Nathanael West."

. . . Sleeping with her is like sleeping with a knife in one's groin.' " (P. 84.) Miss Lonelyhearts is therefore like a child with parents so vicious and so unhappy that identifying with either sex is impossible. And, conversely, identifying with both is inevitable. He is the child in whom all the destructive and conflicting demands of the parents meet. Unless he can reconcile the sexes to each other, they will destroy themselves and him. His own sexual behavior exhibits the same duality of active cruelty and passive suffering. With both Mary Shrike and Betty, for example, he is sometimes as compulsively destructive as Shrike. Sexuality therefore arouses in Miss Lonelyhearts both personal terror and moral horror. His acceptance of "castration" at the moment of conversion is a fantasy of deliverance, not a resignation to loss.

There is, in the saint's vision, no real love but divine love, no real life but eternal life. When God is withdrawn, only deadness remains. Miss Lonelyhearts muses upon "how dead the world is . . . a world of doorknobs" (p. 39), and he dreams of playing the redeemer and bringing the doorknobs to life. "At his command, they bled, flowered, spoke" (p. 40). Regeneration is a classic problem. Its important realities here are the fact of Miss Lonelyhearts' condition and the implications of his role. His dilemma is that of a man with a religious vocation—"for him, Christ was the most natural of excitements"—in which he cannot believe. He knows that his strongest desire leads only to hysteria, that his deepest tendencies have no outlet except in delusion. The frustrations inherent in this condition alone would explain much of his paralysis, and frustration in general would explain the rest. The alternate deadness and violence in Miss Lonelyhearts are a familiar psychological

state, a state which can be induced by any combination of
unremitting stimulus and thwarted response. It does not
matter what the stimulus is—hunger, repressed homosexuality, physical pain—so long as it is inescapable and unrelieved. Nor does it matter what the barriers are so long as
they are insurmountable. In *Miss Lonelyhearts*, constant
pain and constant thwarting are universal. They are conditions of living, not symptoms of individual neuroses, and
"latent homosexuality" is therefore neither a necessary explanation nor a meaningful definition of Miss Lonelyhearts'
problem. If there is no health in us, diagnosis of specific
pathologies is irrelevant, for the real disease is life itself.
And the classic conversion experience derives from exactly
this perception—that both one's own nature and the nature
of mortal life are composed of irreconcilable contradictions, contradictions which are experienced as sin or inherent evil. There is no escape from these contradictions except by escaping the conditions of mortality. One must be
reborn. The terrible paradox of *Miss Lonelyhearts* is that it
accepts the saint's definition of this life but denies the saint's
alternative to it. This world is indeed corrupt, dead, and
irreconcilably evil, but this world is all there is.

The classic problem of misery is, in *Miss Lonelyhearts*,
combined with a modern corollary—the puerility and exhaustion of all classic responses. The implications of this
corollary are everywhere in West, firmly embodied in each
of the deliberately artificial techniques he employed.

The Comic Strip Novel

I can't do a review of *Miss Lonelyhearts*, but here, at
random, are some of the things I thought when writing it:
As subtitle: "A novel in the form of a comic strip." The

chapters to be squares in which many things happen through one action. The speeches contained in the conventional balloons. I abandoned this idea, but retained some of the comic strip technique: Each chapter instead of going forward in time, also goes backward, forward, up and down in space like a picture. Violent images are used to illustrate commonplace events. Violent acts are left almost bald.—West, "Some Notes on Miss Lonelyhearts."[50]

A novel in the form of a comic strip was not as strange a notion as it may seem. West was always fascinated by painting and caricature,[51] and of course popular art was, in intellectual circles of the twenties, as fashionable as the fox-trot. Carl Van Vechten was exploring Harlem, E. E. Cummings was firing off salutes to burlesque, and Gilbert Seldes was proclaiming that Charlie Chaplin and George Herriman (the creator of Krazy Kat) were the two greatest artists in America.[52] The distinctive forms which emerged—movies and comic strips—were both picture narratives. And the union of word and picture was not limited to popular art. The surrealists often used pictorial representations of literary ideas, and even Rimbaud, according to Verlaine, had formed and titled his *Illuminations* after the cheap colored prints which delighted him.[53]

Another fashionable experiment in picture narrative is now almost forgotten—the wordless "novels" in woodcuts of Lynd Ward. *God's Man* and *Madman's Drum* both

[50] West, "Some Notes on Miss Lonelyhearts," p. 1.

[51] It may even be worth remembering that S. J. Perelman, West's friend and brother-in-law, began as a cartoonist, and that West himself drew the first cover design for his college literary magazine.

[52] Gilbert Seldes, *The Seven Lively Arts*, p. 50.

[53] Louise Varèse, Introduction to *Illuminations and Other Prose Poems*, trans. Louise Varèse, pp. x–xii.

preceded *Miss Lonelyhearts* by three years. Ward was not of course a particularly impressive pioneer. His style was commercial, and *God's Man*[54] is just a banal and melodramatic parable of the artist's fate. *Madman's Drum,*[55] however, is fairly interesting in itself and curiously similar to *Miss Lonelyhearts*. West's description of Miss Lonelyhearts exactly matches the puritan hero's countenance in *Madman's Drum*: "No one could fail to recognize the New England puritan. His forehead was high and narrow. His nose was long and fleshless. His bony chin was shaped and cleft like a hoof." (P. 18.) In one of Ward's woodcuts, the hero is profiled against a shadowed wall where a crucifix hangs, looking very much like Miss Lonelyhearts in his room. In another, a seducer buries his sharp chin in the neck of his victim. Even the plot of *Madman's Drum* bears a general resemblance to the plot of *Miss Lonelyhearts*. Abandoning the religion of his ancestors, the hero successively seeks meaning or happiness in philosophy, astronomy, marriage, fatherhood, social action. He fails disastrously in each attempt and ends by embracing madness.

Ward entirely lacked West's subtlety and comic sense, but his techniques, even when crude, suggest more possibilities than Ward himself explored. He necessarily used the devices which any wordless story must: a plot reduced to allegorical simplicity, stereotyped characters whose fea-

[54] Lynd Ward, *God's Man: A Novel in Woodcuts.*
[55] Lynd Ward, *Madman's Drum: A Novel in Woodcuts.* I have no proof that West knew Ward's books at the time he was writing *Miss Lonelyhearts,* though West's interest in the graphic arts and Ward's prominence at the time make it likely that he did. Ward was a frequent contributor to several periodicals, including *Americana,* whose staff West joined a few months after the publication of *Miss Lonelyhearts.* See Light, p. 103.

tures are exaggerated into masks, and physical actions which become, in the absence of words, violent expressive gestures. He used, that is, the conventions which visual media always use. Grotesque masks and violent action are in the standard repertoire of slapstick and pantomime—of Punch and Judy, circus clowns, Keystone cops. When there are no words, gesture and expression must carry everything; violence becomes a form of ballet. In the semi-wordless medium of the comic strip, however, gesture is discontinuous. Both words and actions are fragmentary and overburdened. Dialogue must be compressed into a single speech which in turn must be squeezed into a balloon; action must be revealed in a snapshot image. Under the double pressure of insufficient words and static pictures, violence again becomes a necessary convention, but now the choreographic action of pantomime must yield to images which are as formal and condensed as hieroglyphs. Cartoon panels typically end with exactly that kind of image—with Snuffy Smith sailing over a fence bearing the print of a mule's hoofs on his rump or with Ignatz bouncing a brick off Krazy Kat. In *Miss Lonelyhearts*, West also used violent images as hieroglyphs. When Shrike buries "his triangular face like the blade of a hatchet in [Miss Farkis'] neck" (p. 33), the image reveals the climax of a particular episode, the sadism inherent in all Shrike's actions, and the destructiveness which pervades sexuality throughout the novel. And of course nearly every episode does end in a revelatory and violent image—the sacrifice of the lamb, the torture of the clean old man, the sexual union of Miss Lonelyhearts and Betty in the country. As West said, "Violent images are used to illustrate commonplace events. Violent acts are left almost bald."

But West did not restrict his pictorial style to violent images or to comic-strip techniques. Miss Lonelyhearts lives by himself in a room that is "as full of shadows as an old steel engraving" (p. 37). When he visits Betty, however, he steps out of the engraving and into a Japanese print.

> She came to the door of her apartment in a crisp, white linen dressing-robe that yellowed into brown at the edges. She held out both her hands to him and her arms showed round and smooth like wood that has been turned by the sea. . . .
> She sat down on a studio couch with her bare legs under and her back straight. Behind her a silver tree flowered in the lemon wall-paper. He remained standing.
> "Betty the Buddha," he said. (Pp. 49 and 51.)

As Betty's composure is shattered, the flat stillness of the Japanese print is also shattered. Silver and yellow and brown yield to an angry red. The flat planes of couch and wall shift to ominous curves. "She had left the couch for a red chair that was swollen with padding and tense with live springs. In the grip of this leather monster, all trace of the serene Buddha disappeared." (Pp. 53–54.)

Throughout the novel, scenic styles change like rapidly shifting stage sets. The sacrifice of the lamb is done with the transfiguring light, the pitiless clarity of outline and color, of Dali or an Italian master.

> As the bright sun outlined the altar rock with narrow shadows, the scene appeared to gather itself for some new violence. . . .
> He crushed [the lamb's] head with a stone and left its carcass to the flies that swarmed around the bloody altar flowers. (Pp. 43–44.)

The empty park, surrounded by granite towers and pierced by phallic shadows, is done in the manner of Giorgio de Chirico; a composite street scene is reminiscent of the early George Grosz.

> Crowds of people moved through the street with a dream-like violence. . . .
> He saw a man who appeared to be on the verge of death stagger into a movie theater that was showing a picture called *Blonde Beauty*. He saw a ragged woman with an enormous goiter pick a love story magazine out of a garbage can and seem very excited by her find. (Pp. 145–46.)

There are dream collages in which the letter writers build Miss Lonelyhearts' name out of "faded photographs, soiled fans, time-tables, playing cards, broken toys, imitation jewelry" (p. 101). At one moment the sky looks "as if it had been rubbed with a soiled eraser" (p. 25); later, it is "canvas-colored and ill-stretched" (p. 104). Doyle's face is "like one of those composite photographs used by screen magazines in guessing contests" (p. 167), and Miss Farkis is drawn like a Thurber cartoon: "She had long legs, thick ankles, big hands, a powerful body, a slender neck and a childish face made tiny by a man's haircut" (p. 28).

Varieties of graphic art are also explicitly introduced into the narrative.

> On the mirror behind the bar hung a poster advertising a mineral water. It showed a naked girl made modest by the mist that rose from the spring at her feet. The artist had taken a great deal of care in drawing her breasts and their nipples stuck out like tiny red hats.
> He tried to excite himself into eagerness by thinking of the play Mary made with her breasts. (P. 79.)
> The walls of the booth were covered with obscene

drawings. He fastened his eyes on two disembodied genitals and gave the operator Burgess 7–7323. (P. 102.)

These graphic images obviously contribute both economy
and vividness. They signal a character's preoccupations and
make explanation of them unnecessary. They also reveal, as
I have already said, one of the characteristic symptoms of
Miss Lonelyhearts' illness: the need to read external reality
as if it were a revelation, to search it for clues. Miss Lonelyhearts' confusion destroys psychic autonomy. He does not
know what to do because he does not even know what he
wants, and he expects his surroundings to supply him with
motives, not just with suitable outlets for them. And his
surroundings do. External reality actually is a revelation. A
society is always revealed by the images it fashions, and in
that sense White Rock posters and phone-booth graffiti are
very efficient forms of art—they express the fantasies of
their creators with admirable sincerity and absolute clarity.
That the fantasies are cheap and dehumanized, alternately
impotent and destructive, does not diminish their importance. They are what the world offers; they define the
context in which Miss Lonelyhearts must live.

At times, West uses graphic styles as explicit substitutes
for exposition and description, relying on the reader's familiarity with the style to establish a mood or attitude. A
quick reference to a room "as full of shadows as an old steel
engraving" relieves him of the burden of drawing his own
pictures. At other times, as in the Grosz-like street scene,
West uses an established style as a guide to himself, not as a
signal to the reader, though of course the reader's response
to the verbal picture may be conditioned by his unconscious familiarity with its graphic sources. Finally, the sense
of artificiality which these techniques produce is a part of

the novel's strategy. Miss Lonelyhearts' case is "classical." He, like the other characters in the novel, is an archetype vulgarized into a stereoytpe, and West's graphic parodies underscore both the timelessness and the banality of his role. The role has been played so often that it has become as formal as a minuet. Its lines are familiar, its gestures predictable, its settings stylized into stage sets. For the actors in this drama, triteness is inescapable; their world is as artificial and as sharply bounded as a picture in a frame.

Ritual Theater

I have joyously shut myself up in the solitary domain where the mask holds sway, wholly made up of violence, light, and brilliance. To me the mask means freshness of tone, acute expression, sumptuous decor, great unexpected gestures, unplanned movements, exquisite turbulence.— James Ensor[56]
What Ensor did that was distinctive was to emphasize the mask in its temporary and dangling detachment from man, killing the actor and giving life to the mask. Masks superseded their wearers and virtually had a life of their own and in giving them such a life, Ensor seemed to recapture the transfigured spirit in which masks were regarded by primitive tribes.—Josephine Herbst[57]

West's use of graphic styles inevitably merges with his equally explicit use of theatrical devices. The mask is fundamental to both. Ensor's remarks reveal some of the mask's logic, and Josephine Herbst's comments on Ensor—

---

[56] Paul Haesaerts and James Ensor, *Ensor*, p. 163. Ensor's paintings— *Masks Confronting Death* and *The Entry of Christ into Brussels* are among the more famous—often combine vivid theatricality with a grotesque sense of carnival and riot.
[57] Josephine Herbst, "Hunter of Doves," p. 313.

comments made with West in mind—reveal a good deal
more. The mask is a fate, the formal expression of a role
which obliterates the man who must assume it. It is the face
of a destiny.

Miss Lonelyhearts is given no other name. The name is
his mask, and it is created for him. His passivity is that of an
actor confronted with a role. The part is dictated by the
pressure of mass suffering and by the cynical fraud of his
employers, and if he plays it at all he must play it according
to the script. But the role is both unplayable and unavoid-
able. Miss Lonelyhearts cannot evade it because every attempted escape throws him back upon it. When he tries to
play the gay seducer with Mary Shrike, he is instead forced
to listen to one more litany of pain. His interlude with Fay
Doyle involves him in the hopeless troubles of Peter Doyle,
and even Fay herself insists upon turning the bedroom into
a confessional. "The life out of which she spoke was even
heavier than her body. It was as if a gigantic, living Miss
Lonelyhearts letter in the shape of a paper weight had been
placed on his brain" (p. 109). And mockery is as inescapable as misery. When Miss Lonelyhearts seriously tries to
preach a message, he discovers that his lines have been
written by Shrike, and the scene collapses into farce. His
date with Mary perfectly illustrates the double pressure
upon him. She denies him as a lover and forces him to play
the priest, and then Shrike converts the role into a sinister
joke in which he serves only to excite Shrike's wife for
Shrike's gratification. The mask is unalterable. It is an involuntary disguise, an involuntary cheat—even the sex of this
Redeemer is a fraud—and its falseness degrades both actor
and audience.

Stage metaphors are everywhere in West. In his dream,
Miss Lonelyhearts automatically adopts a theatrical image

to express the fantasy of regeneration. "He found himself on the stage of a crowded theater. He was a magician who did tricks with doorknobs. At his command, they bled, flowered, spoke." (P. 40.) When he rages at Betty, stage mannerisms cripple even his anger. "He began to shout at her, accompanying his shouts with gestures that were too appropriate, like those of an old-fashioned actor." And he concludes: " 'What's the matter, Sweetheart? . . . Didn't you like the performance?' " (Pp. 53–54.) The same banal theatricalism destroys his attempt to preach love to the Doyles: "He tried again by becoming hysterical. 'Christ is love,' he screamed at them. It was a stage scream, but he kept on." (P. 182.) And Miss Lonelyhearts' playacting is complemented by Shrike's "dead pan" performances, by Betty's "wide-eyed little mother act" (p. 117), by Mary Shrike's "formal, impersonal gestures" and "cleanly mechanical . . . pantomime" (p. 88). Betty "unconsciously" exaggerates her "little-girl-in-a-party-dress air" (p. 202), and, upon entering El Gaucho, Mary's movements immediately become "languorous and full of abandon" (p. 86).

In *Miss Lonelyhearts* the world is indeed a stage, but the script is banal and the actors are all bad. Shrike's "dead pan" mask, for example, identifies him with the great god Pan,[58]

[58] Light has noticed the identification with Pan, but I think he has misunderstood its significance. He says: "In Shrike, *Pan* is dead, and Shrike is identified with the new mechanical world based on the emotionless physical sciences. These sciences, in their purest form, exist in the "triangles" of mathematics, and these triangles are symbolized in the novel by the triangular, hatchet-like face of Shrike. These triangles, representing the physical sciences with their tendency to destroy the world of spirit, perpetually bury themselves, as Shrike does, in the neck of mankind." (Light, p. 82.) Light's interpretation here seems to me both strained and irrelevant.

Since these remarks were written, the Pan theme has been lengthily discussed in Robert Andreach's "Nathanael West's *Miss Lonelyhearts*: Between the Dead Pan and the Unborn Christ," pp. 251–60.

and his performance is even more grotesque than Miss Lonelyhearts' imitation of Christ. Pan is not incarnated in Shrike, only embalmed. The vitality of nature is here reduced to the mechanical frenzies and artificial shrieks of a puppet. As his butcher-bird name implies, Shrike retains only the murderousness of the Bacchic orgies, not the creative power. The spokesman for fleshly love is just a killer who cannot even excite his own wife—as impotent as he is destructive. And the other masks are equally classical and equally grotesque—a *magna mater* who "looks like a police captain," a "Virgin" Mary who is a frigid and impure tease, a chaste nymph who believes in advertising and who thinks that "it must steady [Miss Lonelyhearts] to look at a buffalo" (p. 134). In the world of *Miss Lonelyhearts*, all gods are dead. And the deadness of these alternatives to the redeemer role intensifies the pressure upon Miss Lonelyhearts to make his part come alive.

The theatrical metaphor defines the real basis of West's psychology. Behavior is expressive gesture, the attempt to release or fulfill a compulsion whose origins remain obscure. The problem of *Miss Lonelyhearts* is that the compulsion remains alive but the expressive forms have died. All attempts at love or dignity fail. They are puerile gestures which refuse to express real emotion, trite expressions which have become meaningless through repetition. To Miss Lonelyhearts, sex itself is no longer an instinct; it is just another gesture that the mind makes, an irrelevance. Instinctual life manifests itself only in the universal fact of suffering. The letters are depressingly alike, and even Shrike's dead-pan mockery suddenly breaks, letting "pain actually [creep] into his voice" (p. 84). There is, therefore, no escape in comedy. The compulsion can no more be

controlled than fulfilled, and every joke, as in the episode
of the Clean Old Man, erupts into violence. Only dreams
are left. Under the combined pressure of his own sickness
and the desires of all his readers, Miss Lonelyhearts attempts to make the Christ dream come true. The sexual
ambiguity of his name is inherent in the role itself. He is the
embodiment of all dreams—of Doyle's desire for a friend,
of Mrs. Doyle's desire for a lover, of Betty's wish for a
husband, of Shrike's need for a foil.

What of the alternative that Betty represents? It is not an
alternative way of life but an alternative script, a script so
banal that only Betty can take it seriously.

> More than two months had passed since he had sat with
> her on this same couch and had asked her to marry him.
> Then she had accepted him and they had planned their life
> after marriage, his job and her gingham apron, his slippers
> beside the fireplace and her ability to cook. He had
> avoided her since. He did not feel guilty; he was merely
> annoyed at having been fooled into thinking that such a
> solution was possible. (Pp. 51–52.)

The solution is not possible because it is not real—Betty is
largely just an animated cliché. Miss Lonelyhearts can only
ignore her script, or try to violate it, or submit to it. The
last alternative is of course what Betty expects. She is as full
of cues as a prompter, and she expects them to be followed.
When they go to bed in the country, "He fondled her, but
when she said that she was a virgin, he let her alone and
went to sleep" (p. 138). The next day, he responds to her
"childishly sexual" gesture by vaulting a porch rail and
coupling with her on the grass. In each case, he has just
taken his cue from Betty, first by playing the Gentleman
and then by playing the Impassioned Lover. And in his

final hysteria, of course, Miss Lonelyhearts slips into Betty's script with total ease.

> He begged the party dress to marry him, saying all the things it expected to hear, all the things that went with strawberry sodas and farms in Connecticut. He was just what the party dress wanted him to be: simple and sweet, whimsical and poetic, a trifle collegiate yet very masculine. (P. 205.)

The irony, of course, is that Miss Lonelyhearts becomes just what Betty wanted him to be by entirely ceasing to be human. In his delusional hysteria, he can ignore reality, including the reality of himself, and perfectly embody Betty's fantasy. He can be the man of her dreams.

The banality of Betty's script is not merely funny. Triteness confers no immunity to pain, and Betty's incomprehension is nearly as destructive to her as it is to Miss Lonelyhearts. Her belief in the curative power of nature leaves her pregnant and husbandless. She is miserable, and she was not prepared for misery—her belief in the script was, after all, as sincere as it was stupid, and her belief was all she had. Without it, she is simply vulnerable. For the Bettys of this world, reality can only destroy innocence, not enlighten it.

Betty's "soft helplessness" does not, of course, prevent her from imposing a role upon Miss Lonelyhearts. With her, as with everyone else, he must passively submit to the expectations of a fantasy, not pursue the implications of his own nature. And Betty's expectations conflict with other expectations. To accept her demands is to deny those of the letter writers. Miss Lonelyhearts' role is, in other words, composed of so many contradictions that it can only destroy the actor. A redeemer has to be everybody's darling; he is the focus of all desire, but in the real world desires are

often antagonistic. It is safe for opposing armies to pray to
the same god only so long as the god does not unequivo-
cally answer either prayer or make the mistake of coming
down to earth. If he does, the god is sure to be destroyed
and both armies are sure to feel cheated. Suffering is not
impersonal; it derives from the things people do to people.
To sympathize with one victim is often to betray or to
repudiate another, and at the climax of his mission Miss
Lonelyhearts faces exactly that dilemma. He is the emotional focus for both Fay and Peter Doyle. The contradictions inherent in this double role can be resolved only by
unsexing himself and by replacing Eros with Agape—only,
that is, by transcending the human and invoking the divine.
But he is not divine. The contradictions in his role are the
contradictions inherent in life. To Fay Doyle, the embodied life force, sexless love is no more attractive than suicide.
She can neither understand it nor respond to it, and the
Agape Miss Lonelyhearts preaches is therefore, to her, as
irrelevant as it is unreal. Miss Lonelyhearts has no message.
He cannot resolve the contradictions of this life; he can
only deny them and escape into delusion and death.

Ménage à trois

To discuss roles is to raise, inevitably, the problem of archetypal interpretation. Such interpretation carries with it so
many dangers—so many temptations to let the eyes drift
out of focus and see only the shimmering and indistinct
phantoms of universal myth—that I am uneasy about attempting it. But I shall. And therefore I must say in advance
that the discussion necessarily ignores innumerable details
which are important, and that I offer it with even more
than the usual apologies for oversimplification.

The triad of Doyle, Mrs. Doyle, and Miss Lonelyhearts recalls the similar grouping of Wilson, Myrtle Wilson, and Gatsby in *The Great Gatsby*. In both novels, a crippled or devitalized cuckold is married to a vulgar but vital woman, and in both novels the cuckold mistakenly kills the "spiritual" hero in revenge for his wife's betrayal. The similarities do not end there. Gatsby and Miss Lonelyhearts are both priestly figures, celebrants of an eternal dream which refuses to come true, and both pursue their dreams in a vulgarized world whose image is the waste land. Both destinies are tragicomic and both heroes are holy fools. They take their dreams seriously and are destroyed by them. The Cinderella dream of American success produces only a self-made gangster with elegant manners and gorgeous illusions; the Christ dream is enacted by a lovelorn columnist whose crucifixion is squalid and pointless. Even the styles of Fitzgerald and West are related. Both unite an acute ear for vulgar speech with an instinct for poetry and comedy. I think West learned from Fitzgerald, and I think the grotesque fate of Miss Lonelyhearts was a conscious echo of Gatsby's equally grotesque end. But the differences are important too. Characteristically, West's world is harsher than Fitzgerald's. The compulsions of his characters are more desperate, the logic of his plot is more relentless, the implications of his vision are more ominous and insistent. Acute misery, not unsatisfied yearning, is the universal human sensation in *Miss Lonelyhearts*. Myrtle Wilson's vulgar vitality becomes Fay Doyle's sordid brutality, and the Keatsian sensuousness of Fitzgerald's prose yields to West's vivid and repellent hieroglyphs. There are no "green lights" in *Miss Lonelyhearts*, no "enchanted objects" at all. White Rock posters and phone-booth graffiti are what confront the dreamer; Romance is not even a plausible illusion, and Beauty is not even a deceptive appearance. Nor is there a Nick Carraway to supply a mitigating elegy. The painful farce of Miss Lonelyhearts' death is unrelieved by any surviving dreamer or any surviving dream.

Miss Lonelyhearts' involvement with the Doyles is matched by his involvement with the Shrikes, but this second triad inverts the terms of the first. Shrike is as vicious as Doyle is helpless, and Mary is as frigid as Mrs. Doyle is aggressive. The two triads define the novel's opposed forces with almost diagrammatic neatness. In Shrike's proper genealogy, Chillingworth and Iago and the Pardoner would figure at least as prominently as Pan. He is parasitic, fond of manipulation, eager to subvert both spiritual and fleshly desires until they collapse into jokes of his own contriving. He is therefore an enemy of life, not its celebrant. And his marriage to the life-denying Mary is far more appropriate than bizarre. The Doyle's marriage is equally appropriate. The "moon driven" Fay's avatars range from Astarte to Molly Bloom, and her "sea-moan" of desire is surely a deliberate parody of Molly's tidal flow of reverie and passion. What is the point? Fay embodies that mindless force of nature which is doomed by its own voracity. The Fay Doyles of this world will never be content with a "shrimp of a cripple" (p. 112) who is "all dried up" (p. 108); yet the Fay Doyles will give birth to, among other things, an endless number of such cripples. Nature is ruthlessly indifferent to its own products—and incapable of being satisfied by them. The marriage is therefore a metaphoric irony. It inseparably yokes the life force and its victims, demonstrating that the "marriage" is both disastrous and indissoluble.

As the common point in both triads, Miss Lonelyhearts is the natural target for the destruction latent in each. The Doyles (and, behind them, the letter writers) exert the pressure of unappeasable desire, while Shrike destroys every possible outlet for it. Even Mary's sexuality becomes part of Shrike's repertoire, as fraudulent as any dream of art or the South Seas. Shrike manipulates her frigidity even while he suffers from it. Mary is a tease, perpetually arousing desire and then denying it, and the denouement of her flirtation with Miss Lonelyhearts is exactly like the denouement of each of Shrike's parodies—it reveals that the promised satisfaction is just a joke.

Marriage is a conventional symbol of reconciliation, but the symbolic triads in *Miss Lonelyhearts* unite only to make destruction complete. Shrike and Mary reflect the perversion of nature under the dominance of a crippled male principle—a parasitic and manipulative intellect—and the Doyles reflect the cruelty of nature under the dominance of a brutalized female principle—a desire as formless and devouring as the sea.

Depression and the Imagery of Disorder

Having touched on the archetypal, I must now turn to the topical. *Miss Lonelyhearts* was, despite its mythic outlines and literary allusions, very much the product of immediate social realities. The double theme of helpless suffering and fraudulent cures is always relevant, and in the depression year of 1933 it had a special edge. More than the stock market had boomed in the twenties. That decade saw the real emergence of the tabloids, of feature-length films, of radio soap operas—of all those new media which helped inflate cheap emotions and sell meretricious dreams.[59] In *Miss Lonelyhearts*, the boom has collapsed. Dreams are as void as worthless stocks, and depression is a universal fact. Even Shrike's poses are threadbare. He neatly illustrates—and parodies—that blend of pseudo-dada and pseudo-pagan which formed the fashionable costume of so many intellectuals in the twenties. Like the dadaists, he sneeringly rejects the "new thomistic synthesis" (p. 29) in favor of adding-machine cults and lovelorn columnists. Like the pagans, he identifies himself as a "fleshly lover" and a disciple of Pan. And Pan, of course, lurked in half the stage shrubbery and novelistic fancies of the period. Gilbert Seldes even discovered him reincarnated in the person of Al Jolson.[60]

The depression gave West more than a metaphor to express the economy of dreams. At the Sutton Hotel, he was in intimate contact with some of its representative victims. Josephine Herbst remembers hearing West tell appalling stories about the lives of his hotel guests, lives which seemed to fascinate and depress him,[61] and Lillian Hellman recalls that she frequently helped West steam open the guests' mail.[62] The letters in *Miss Lonelyhearts* may owe more than a little of their authenticity to this practice.[63]

[59] Lovelorn columnists were also extremely popular. Beatrice Fairfax's column in the *New York Journal* sometimes elicited 1,400 letters a day. "Beatrice Fairfax," *The Reader's Encyclopedia of American Literature*, ed. Max J. Herzberg (New York: Thomas Y. Crowell Co., 1962).

[60] Seldes, p. 191.

[61] Herbst, "Hunter of Doves," p. 321.

[62] Lillian Hellman, "The Art of the Theater I."

[63] Presumably, however, most of the Sutton's guests were originally of a higher socio-economic class than the letter writers in *Miss Lonelyhearts*. Perhaps the pervasive tone of failure and collapse among the Sutton's guests was more influential on West than the actual letters they received.

And West was, I suspect, instinctively responsive to the conditions of depression. For him, collapse was perhaps less a shock than a natural confirmation of what he had always secretly known. The psychology of Miss Lonelyhearts himself carries a conviction which could not have been supplied by any synthesis of borrowed case histories.

He read [the letter] for the same reason that an animal tears at a wounded foot: to hurt the pain (p. 148).

Miss Lonelyhearts felt as he had felt years before, when he had accidentally stepped on a small frog. Its spilled guts had filled him with pity, but when its suffering had become real to his senses, his pity had turned to rage and he had beaten it frantically until it was dead (p. 69).

These comments bear the authority of personal experience, not that of the textbook. They give the classical case history a vivid actuality which no psychological theory could supply.

West constantly united direct perception with traditional material. He could borrow freely because he didn't have to, because he understood the materials he borrowed so well that he could have invented them himself. He obviously saw the links between the Dandy, the Dostoevskian criminal, the Saint, the Fool, the Sacrificial Hero, and certain instincts in himself. He fused them all into the character of Miss Lonelyhearts. And both life and literature are full of Bettys, of Shrikes and Mrs. Shrikes, of Doyles and Mrs. Doyles. Their ancestors are found throughout European literature, but they are recognizably modern and American. West's synthesis of classic types is, therefore, at once a clarification of and comment upon contemporary roles.

"Clarity" is a key word here. West's control of his sources is perfectly illustrated in the compression of his style. His parodies are always briefer than the originals, always reduced to their essential features and then fitted smoothly into a context of other parodies which interact as inevitably as chemical elements. Unlike the cryptic allusions of *The Waste Land*, West's generic parodies therefore require no footnotes. They are familiar and intelligible whether or not we recognize their particular sources.

West's images show the same lucidity. Miss Lonelyhearts' "almost insane sensitiveness to order" (p. 48) is both a classic symptom of preconversion psychology and a metaphor which expresses the problem of the novel. The problem is explicitly stated: "Man has a tropism for order. . . . The physical world has a tropism for disorder, entropy" (pp. 115–16). The contrast is between meaning and chaos, between coherent form and disintegration, between spiritual life and the "mechanics of decay." It is embodied in a succession of images. In a moment of drunken beatitude, Miss Lonelyhearts dreams of children dancing in formal patterns, "square replacing oblong and being replaced by circle" (pp. 64–65). He visits Betty because "she had often made him feel that when she straightened his tie, she straightened much more" (pp. 48–49). But the arbitrary limits of Betty's order make it useless. The Japanese print cannot survive Miss Lonelyhearts' intrusion—it is an inadequate form whose serenity depends upon the exclusion of all harsh facts. And when Miss Lonelyhearts tries in fantasy to organize all the junk in a pawn shop window, he uses first a phallus, then a heart, then a diamond, circle, triangle, square, swastika, but "nothing proved definitive and he began to make a gigantic cross. When the cross became too large for the pawnshop, he moved it to the shore of the ocean. There every wave added to his stock faster than he could lengthen its arms." (P. 116.) Images of disorder and the sea steadily build until Miss Lonelyhearts encounters the cripple Doyle, who becomes the test of his mission. "The cripple had a very strange face. His eyes failed to balance; his mouth was not under his nose; his forehead was square and bony; and his round chin was like a forehead in miniature" (p. 167). And of course the grotesquely misshapen Doyle is married to the "tidal, moon-driven" Mrs. Doyle.

The same insistent logic brings other images into final focus. The "flies that swarmed around the bloody altar flowers" (p. 44) in the sacrifice of the lamb reappear in Miss Lonelyhearts' feverish delusion—the crucifix becomes "a bright fly, spinning with quick grace on a background of blood velvet sprinkled with tiny nerve stars" (p. 209). The "stone that had formed in his gut" (p. 25) becomes the "calm and solid" rock (p. 190) of catatonic deadness. The flowering of doorknobs (p. 40) and skeletons (p. 102) culminates in Miss Lonelyhearts' moment of illusory communion with God. "His heart was a rose and in his skull another rose bloomed" (p. 210).

The book has almost no loose ends. Its parodies are so perfectly fused, its images so cleanly ordered, its "artificial" techniques so naturally related to its themes, that it achieves an economy which has not yet been matched in American fiction. It has all the virtues—and some of the limitations—of extreme clarity. Like syllogisms and pictures, tightly constructed novels may achieve coherence at the price of exclusion, and in *Miss Lonelyhearts* human personality is perhaps too much reduced to the common denominator of suffering. Though it is his most perfect novel, *Miss Lonelyhearts* was not West's last word. Misery is not the only important aspect of mass privation, and mockery and compassion are not the only responses to it. In *The Day of the Locust*, West pursued many of the implications which remain.

A Cool Million:

"SURFEIT OF SHODDY"

Perhaps the first thing to be said about *A Cool Million* is that it is not very good. By itself, it has no more claim to our attention than several dozen properly forgotten books of the thirties. But of course it does not stand by itself. Viewed as a transition from *Miss Lonelyhearts* to *The Day of the Locust*, it exhibits embryonic triumphs as well as temporary lapses.

The burlesque in *A Cool Million* is consistently heavy and only intermittently funny. Worse, it largely isolates the reader from the force of its satire. In a world so dominated by moronic gullibility, a reader can neither identify with the characters nor feel much complicity in the folly and evil they represent. West's typical mixed vision is here entirely absent. It is replaced by an odd jumble of travesties, few of which are impressive and all of which combine to destroy even the effect of simple bitterness. The book is as crude as a political cartoon but not as coherent. The Alger parodies involve so much coyly deliberate bad writing, so many ponderous winks to the reader, that *saeva indignatio* is often less apparent than the ubiquitous Wise Guy's smirk.

Perhaps West's choice of targets is itself responsible. Half-witted philosophies deserve to be opposed, but not by simple hyperbole—not, that is, unless the hyperbole is inventive enough and zestful enough to be funny in itself. *A Cool Million* seldom is. The Alger stories it travesties are so ridiculous that they defy parody; burlesque is the only way to handle them, and burlesque, as I have already argued, did not come easily to West. Neither did rapid composition. *A Cool Million* was hurriedly written at a time when West was trying to escape the hotel business,[1] and the haste shows. His performance suggests an unresolved confusion of intentions which committed him to a series of mistakes he did not have time to correct. He hoped, for example, to make enough money to live by his writing, but his choice of methods was disastrously bad. The book was a commercial failure, as even West should have known it would be. Personal loyalties may also have confused him. *A Cool Million* is dedicated to S. J. Perelman, and it sometimes imitates, largely without success, the techniques of flamboyant travesty which Perelman has specialized in.[2] And West

---

[1] Light, p. 128.

[2] West's and Perelman's work exhibit many similarities, including a number of shared phrases. In "Entered as Second-class Matter," for example, Perelman speaks of "Shav-Komfy, the shave-secret of the Aztecs," (*The Most of S. J. Perelman* [New York: Simon and Schuster, 1958], p. 100), while in *The Day of the Locust*, Tod Hackett visits a temple where "Brain-Breathing, the Secret of the Aztecs" is taught. And in a recent interview, Perelman (like the newspapermen in *Miss Lonelyhearts*) complained of lady writers "with three-barreled names" and compared Hollywood to a Sargasso Sea (as West does in *The Day of the Locust*). See "The Art of Fiction: S. J. Perelman." I do not think any important conclusions can be drawn from these similarities. West and Perelman were friends from their college years, and they probably both drew on phrases, ideas, and jokes which were part of the repertoire of their friendship.

may have felt some desire to express his political sympathies and join the crusade against fascism. Shagpoke Whipple's Leather Shirts do, after all, represent a specific evil and a specific stupidity. Whether one chooses to fight it or laugh at it, one's response is uncomplicated. Unfortunately, such an attitude is as unenlightening as it is simple. In *A Cool Million*, fascism is only a stupidity or only a threat—a stupidity which is not even made credible, as it is in *The Day of the Locust*, by any sense of one's own secret participation in it.

As nearly everyone recognizes, the basic strategy of *A Cool Million* is to impose the pattern of *Candide* upon Horatio Alger materials. The strategy is, I think, clearly a mistake. It immediately sacrifices the qualities of style upon which *Candide* depends. It also abandons West's own gift for parody—the condensed and suggestive summary—in favor of extended imitation. Perhaps unfortunately, the imitation is quite accurate. It reproduces the circumlocutions, the wooden descriptions, and the moralizing digressions of its Alger originals with depressing faithfulness. It also reproduces the rudimentary formula of the Alger plot: a poor but honest farm boy with a widowed mother goes forth to seek his fortune.[3] Obviously, such a hero should succeed through Luck and Pluck. But he doesn't. His pluck is only persistence in stupidity, and his luck is all bad. " 'Jail is his first reward. Poverty his second. Violence is his third. Death is his last.' "[4] The Alger success story is turned on its

---

[3] These are not, of course, the only stock properties. The threatened foreclosure and the encounters with the Bully, the Sharper, and the Intemperate Spendthrift are all familiar from Alger.

[4] *A Cool Million* in *The Complete Works of Nathanael West*. Subsequent references are to the same edition and are indicated by page numbers in parentheses.

head. With Shagpoke Whipple as his Pangloss and Betty
Prail as his Cunegonde, the American Candide lurches
through a series of disasters without acquiring wealth or
wisdom. He is simply destroyed. Indeed, the process of his
"dismantling" is at times even more reminiscent of Sade's
Justine than it is of *Candide*.

Lem's adventures are repetitive in several ways. Abandoning irony, West attacks some of his favorite targets
with a bludgeon. The refrain of "no morality, only medicine" in *Miss Lonelyhearts* is loudly echoed by Warden
Purdy, who believes that "the sick are never guilty," and
that all criminals are "merely sick" (p. 166). His therapy is,
of course, worse than punishment. He pulls all Lem's teeth
and forces him through a series of cold showers which end
in pneumonia. And the Betty of *Miss Lonelyhearts* becomes Betty Prail, a girl who suffers rape as monotonously
as Lem suffers disfigurement but who remains unalterably
an ingenue. Other repetitions seem curiously pointless.
Samuel Perkins, the artist of odors in *Balso Snell*, is now a
flashy youth who attempts to lead Lem astray. *Miss Lonelyhearts* has a Ned Gates, and a Mr. Gates appears in *A
Cool Million*. West's use of names is, throughout the book,
constantly allusive and often puzzling. Many names are
obvious tags or obvious jokes—"Lemuel" suggests "Lemuel Gulliver," and both "Prail" and "Kanurani" are appropriate, if obscene, puns.[5] But there are still other plays
on names which are apparently deliberate but apparently
without literary motive. Why, for example, should West
have given the first name and last initial of his former

---

[5] "Prail" is probably a compound of "prat," "tail," and "frail," and the
sodomitic Prince Kanurani's name is a blend of "can" and "your ani."

fiancée to one of the whores in Wu Fong's house?[6] And why should he have given his own first name and last initial to Nathan "Shagpoke" Whipple? The answer would seem to lie in private jokes or private resentments. Like some other details of *A Cool Million*, these allusions suggest that West's attitude toward his materials may have been muddied by irrelevant motives.

As Lem's story progresses, the Alger form relaxes enough to permit other parodies. The mining camp sequence, with its blend of the picturesque and the bathetic, is pure Bret Harte:

> Once more the deep hush of the primeval forest descended on the little clearing, making peaceful what had been a scene of wild torment and savage villainy. A squirrel began to chatter hysterically in a treetop and from somewhere along the brook came the plash of a rising trout. Birds sang.
> Suddenly the birds were still. The squirrel fled from the tree in which he had been gathering pine cones. Something was moving behind the woodpile. Jake Raven was not dead after all. (Pp. 230–31.)

Whipple's Leather Shirts, with their coonskin caps and squirrel rifles, mock the Davy Crockett–Daniel Boone myth, and Lem's assassination in the theater obviously recalls the shooting of Lincoln.

There is, however, still another kind of parody which is

---

[6] The girl in Wu Fong's house is Alice Sweethorne. West's engagement to Alice Shepherd lasted for three years, ending shortly after the publication of *Miss Lonelyhearts*. Miss Shepherd was Catholic, and John Sanford has suggested that the engagement foundered primarily on the religious difference. See Light, pp. 73–74. For an interesting fictionalized account of the engagement and of West, see Josephine Herbst's "Hunter of Doves."

as unrelated to the Alger form as it is important to West's later work. The most distinctive feature of *A Cool Million* is its meticulous descriptions of American decor. The Pitkin family home is foreclosed so it can be sold to Asa Goldstein, a Fifth Avenue decorator who specializes in "Colonial Exteriors and Interiors" and who moves the house intact to his show windows, carefully preserving the authenticity of every detail. The same Asa Goldstein is hired to convert Wu Fong's brothel of all nations into a whorehouse museum of Americana—"Pennsylvania Dutch, Old South, Log Cabin Pioneer, Victorian New York, Western Cattle Days, California Monterey, Indian, and Modern Girl" (p. 202). Again, the decoration is meticulously authentic. Betty is installed in a colonial interior with "antimacassars, ships in bottles, carved whalebone, hooked rugs . . . [and a] poster bed with its candlewick spread" (p. 170). Her dress

> had a full waist made with a yoke and belt, a gored skirt, long, but not too long to afford a very distinct view of a well-turned ankle and a small, shapely foot encased in a snowy cotton stocking and a low-heeled black slipper. The material of the dress was chintz—white ground with a tiny brown figure—finished at the neck with a wide white ruffle. On her hands she was made to wear black silk mitts with half-fingers. Her hair was worn in a little knot on the top of her head, and one thick short curl was kept in place by a puff-comb on each side of her face. (P. 170.)

The other girls are costumed and housed with equal appropriateness.

> Mary Judkins from Jugtown Hill, Arkansas. Her walls were lined with oak puncheons chinked with mud. Her mattress was stuffed with field corn and covered by a

buffalo robe. There was real dirt on her floors. She was dressed in homespun, butternut stained, and wore a pair of men's boots.

Patricia Van Riis from Gramercy Park, Manhattan, New York City. Her suite was done in the style known as Biedermeier. The windows were draped with thirty yards of white velvet apiece and the chandelier in her sitting room had over eight hundred crystal pendants attached to it. She was dressed like an early "Gibson Girl." . . .

Princess Roan Fawn from Two Forks, Oklahoma Indian Reservation, Oklahoma. Her walls were papered with birch bark to make it look like a wigwam and she did business on the floor. Except for a necklace of wolf's teeth, she was naked under her bull's-eye blanket. (Pp. 203–204.)

The same relentless "authenticity" is carried into the cuisine.

When a client visited Lena Haubengrauber, it was possible for him to eat roast groundhog and drink Sam Thompson rye. While with Alice Sweethorne, he was served sow belly with grits and bourbon. In Mary Judkins' rooms he received, if he so desired, fried squirrel and corn liquor. In the suite occupied by Patricia Van Riis, lobster and champagne wine were the rule. The patrons of Powder River Rose usually ordered mountain oysters and washed them down with forty-rod. And so on down the list: while with Dolores O'Riely, tortillas and prune brandy from the Imperial Valley; while with Princess Roan Fawn, baked dog and firewater; while with Betty Prail, fish chowder and Jamaica rum. Finally, those who sought the favors of the "Modern Girl," Miss Cobina Wiggs, were regaled with tomato and lettuce sandwiches and gin. (Pp. 204–205.)

Wu Fong's inspiration is, of course, the Buy American campaign of the Hearst papers. His switch from an interna-

tional theme to vintage Americana offers a caustic, and
appropriate, comment on the venal exploitation of patriot-
ism. It is also a triumph of merchandising. Like a true
American businessman, Wu Fong knows that he should sell
the sizzle not the steak, the package not the product. Sexual
gratification has little to do with Wu Fong's business; like
other retailers, he panders fundamentally to the lust for
novelty and illusion. His elaborate fakes are only an elegant
variation of the vulgar, manufactured junk exhibited in the
Chamber of American Horrors, "objects whose distinction
lay in the great skill with which their materials had been
disguised. Paper had been made to look like wood, wood
like rubber, rubber like steel, steel like cheese, cheese like
glass, and, finally, glass like paper." (P. 239.)

American life offers enough synthetic horrors and
enough skillful merchandising of meretricious dreams to
give a writer like West all the material he needed. But he
had a literary source too. Behind Wu Fong's whorehouse
and the Chambers of American Horrors lurks a familiar
shadow—that of Joris-Karl Huysmans. Des Esseintes, the
hero of *Against the Grain,* devoted most of his time to
illustrating his own maxim that artifice is the "distinctive
mark of human genius." His private retreat—a room within
a room whose window had been replaced by a glass tank—
was entirely worthy of the combined talents of Wu Fong
and Asa Goldstein. It featured

a system of pipes and conduits that enabled the tank to be
emptied and refilled with fresh water, and then by pour-
ing in a few drops of coloured essences, he could enjoy at
his pleasure all the tints, green or grey, opaline or silvery,
that real rivers assume. . . .

This done, he could picture himself in the 'tween-decks

of a brig as he gazed curiously at a shoal of ingenious
mechanical fishes that were wound up and swam by clock-
work past the port-hole window and got entangled in
artificial water-weeds; at other times, as he inhaled the
strong smell of tar with which the room had been impreg-
nated before he entered it, he would examine a series of
coloured lithographs on the walls, of the sort one sees in
packet-boat offices and shipping agencies. . . .
In the last resort, he could turn his gaze upon a litter of
fishing rods, brown tanned nets, rolls of russet-coloured
sails, a miniature anchor made of cork painted black. . . .
By these means he could procure himself, without ever
stirring from home . . . all the sensations of a long voy-
age.[7]

This is funny enough, and the seriousness with which
Huysmans treats it makes it even funnier. West's parody is,
in part, just a natural exploitation of the comic possibilities
in the tastes of the dandy. But the parody also contains a
discovery, a discovery which is only partly explored in *A
Cool Million* but which West developed in *The Day of the
Locust*. The discovery is this: the tastes of the dandy are
the tastes of American vulgarity. The aesthete whose whole
career is an exercise in contempt for the masses is actually
indistinguishable from them. He shares their lust for illusion, for elaborate artifice and novelty, and his irritable
ennui is only an attenuated form of their latent violence.
His psychology, like theirs, derives from frustration, irritation, and exhaustion; and his desires, like theirs, issue forth
in dreams and fitful destructive acts. In Huysmans, West

[7] Huysmans, *Against the Grain*, pp. 100–101. Daniel Aaron has briefly
suggested that "the meticulous way in which [West] delineates the
atrocious reminds us of Huysmans," but, so far as I know, West's direct
borrowings from Huysmans have not previously been noticed. See Aaron,
"Waiting for the Apocalypse."

discovered a method which he elaborated into a metaphor. The method concentrates on the decor of illusions and it leads naturally to the half-metaphoric image of the museum—of Americana whorehouses, dream dumps, chambers of synthetic American horrors. In *A Cool Million*, the museum is, I think, the real focus of West's literary instincts. It even revives, if only briefly, the vivid precision of his usual style.

> The hall which led to the main room of the "inanimate" exhibit was lined with sculptures in plaster. Among the most striking of these was a Venus de Milo with a clock in her abdomen, a copy of Power's "Greek Slave" with elastic bandages on all her joints, a Hercules wearing a small, compact truss. (P. 239.)

But the museum remains a static digression within an Horatio Alger plot. It is never really fused with the book's controlling pattern, because it is naturally distinct from it. The museum displays the visual symbols of American illusion in an enclosed space. It is really an alternate method, not just an addition, to the picaresque journey and its revelations of deceit through multiple incidents strung out in time. And the museum was far more natural to West than the picaresque plot. In *The Day of the Locust*, he used its possibilities to explore the natural museum of southern California, a world which lures representative victims of every dream. Hollywood is, in West's hands, both a dream factory and a dream dump, the source and termination of all those manufactured visions which flicker through the lives of people who, at last, come to California, but only to die.

The Day
of the Locust:
VENUS IN THE PROMISED LAND

Artists and Actors

The Day of the Locust can be read as a statement of what must follow the failure of the Christ dream. In this novel, even the pseudo-saviour is missing. Miss Lonelyhearts is dead, and so is his dream. Tod Hackett, who takes his place, specifically says that "he had never set himself up as a healer,"[1] referring to himself instead as a Jeremiah, a prophet of the coming destruction (p. 78). In the background, of course, we have a variety of lunatic churches-militant, symbolized by that leader of the "screwballs and screwboxes," Dr. Know-All Pierce-All (p. 165). And the helpless sufferers who sought redemption in *Miss Lonelyhearts* have become, in *The Day of the Locust*, an embittered mob which seeks revenge. There is a corresponding change in tone. That form of pity which Miss Lonelyhearts represented and that form of mockery which Shrike represented have both largely disappeared. The nearest thing to a Shrike figure is Claude Estee, a "master of comic rhetoric," but he is neither a particularly important character nor a par-

---

[1] *The Day of the Locust* in *Miss Lonelyhearts and The Day of the Locust*, p. 133. Subsequent references are to the same edition and are indicated by page numbers in parentheses.

ticularly caustic mocker. Tod exactly defines the changed tone when he thinks of how Alessandro Magnasco, one of his professed masters, would paint the embittered members of the mob. "He would not satirize them as Hogarth or Daumier might, nor would he pity them. He would paint their fury with respect, appreciating its awful, anarchic power and aware that they had it in them to destroy civilization." (Pp. 109–10.)

The change in tone is matched by a change in pictorial style. Instead of a room that was "as full of shadows as an old steel engraving," we have the careful description of Homer's house; instead of a sky that looked "as if it had been rubbed with a soiled eraser," we have fully painted landscapes. "The edges of the trees burned with a pale violet light and their centers gradually turned from deep purple to black. The same violet piping, like a neon tube, outlined the top of the ugly, hump-backed hills and they were almost beautiful." (P. 3.) An artificial image—the Neon tube—remains, but it is now used to describe the appearance of a real scene, not to transform landscapes into formal stage sets. And, unlike the alternately static and jerkily animated scenes of *Miss Lonelyhearts*, this picture slowly changes while we watch it. The gradual darkening of color here is characteristic of the novel's methods and it signals a basic change in form: *The Day of the Locust* is a motion picture, not a comic strip.

The change in pictorial style also derives in part from the change in central characters: a painter is substituted for a quasi-mystical priest. Though he too searches external reality for clues, Tod does not expect it to confront him with ready-made revelations. His clues are the symbols he can fashion into pictures of his own. He is analytical, not hallucinatory; attentive to detail, not receptive to suggestion. And the choice of such a viewpoint character suggests, in West, that respect toward his materials which Tod attributes to Magnasco—a determination to forego the distortions of pity and satire, a conviction that the world which confronts him is so "truly monstrous" (p. 4) that clear vision, not imagination, is the artist's fundamental tool.

A painter's style defines, of course, the way things should be seen. In *The Day of the Locust*, it is both more tentative and more exact than in *Miss Lonelyhearts*. The confident manipulation of engravings, Japanese prints, and Chirico-like visions yields to Tod's explicit but uncertain references to those painters who can guide him. He thinks first of Goya and Daumier (p. 3); then of Rosa, Guardi, and Desiderio (p. 96); and finally, rejecting Hogarth and Daumier, of Magnasco. Yet even Magnasco is inadequate. His manner is perfectly suited to the mob, but it cannot reveal Homer, who is "like one of Picasso's great sterile athletes" (p. 32), nor Faye and Harry Greener, nor that "mechanical drawing" Earle Shoop (p. 66). No single style is any more definitive than the forms Miss Lonelyhearts attempted to impose on the junk in a pawnshop window. The world remains discordant, peopled by natural grotesques who have been further twisted by the influence of stereotypes and bad art. To paint them, one must reveal their banality and their incoherence as types—a movie poster Venus, a clown whose features are carved like a mask, a Picasso athlete, a cowboy with "a two-dimensional face that a talented child might have drawn with a ruler and a compass" (p. 66). Massed behind these figures are Magnasco's fanatics with "countersunk eyes, like the heads of burnished spikes" (p. 110), moving against a background of movie sets and stucco castles and canyons where grass and wild flowers grow. Real poplars shade "brown plaster" rocks (p. 96), and imitation hills collapse under armies of live actors (p. 100). The sense of disjunction in such a world is both comic and violent. It is also convincingly real. *The Day of the Locust* creates its "surrealistic" landscapes out of actual materials.[2] It transfers *A Cool Million*'s meticulous descriptions of decor to a world where illusion is an industry, where fantasies take architectural form and the rubbish of dreams forms "a Sargasso of the imagination" (p. 97). Though its images are slower to focus and its plot lacks the relentless acceleration of *Miss Lonelyhearts*, *The Day of the Locust* has the veracity of acute, wakeful vision, not that of a dream.

West's recurrent theatrical metaphor also shows a new literalness. Faye and Harry and Earle are all actors, actual or aspiring, and their natural audience is that mass of bored and irritable spectators who lurk on every corner. As always in West, the demands of the audience exert a dreadful pressure on the performer. "It was their stare that drove Abe and the others to spin crazily and leap into the air with twisted backs like hooked trout" (p. 5). This is the familiar desperation of Miss Lonelyhearts, forced by the pressure of mass suffering to act an impossible role, or of John Gilson attempting to impress Saniette. "Her casualness excited me so that I became more and more desperate in my performances."[3] In *The Day of the Locust*, the audience pressure is

[2] Light quotes Allan Seager: " 'Having known something of the Hollywood West saw at the time he was seeing it, I am of the opinion that *Locust* was not fantasy imagined, but fantasy seen.' " Light, p. 153.

[3] The connection between Gilson's remarks on acting and the performers in *The Day of the Locust* has been frequently noted. See, for example, Light, pp. 172–73.

boredom, not misery, and the performer's compulsion is to arouse his audience. When Harry Greener, the veteran clown and con man, confronts Homer Simpson, the catatonically inert spectator and victim, he is siezed by an appropriate spasm of involuntary performance.

> Suddenly, like a mechanical toy that had been overwound, something snapped inside of him and he began to spin through his entire repertoire. The effort was purely muscular, like the dance of a paralytic. He jigged, juggled his hat, made believe he had been kicked, tripped, and shook hands with himself. He went through it all in one dizzy spasm, then reeled to the couch and collapsed. (P. 44.)

The scene is comic, but it is also as repellent as the contortions produced by electric shock. And it is nearly indistinguishable from them. In West, the interaction between performer and audience is compulsive and mutually degrading, like mechanical stimulation. It is also the paradigm for all interactions—demagogue and mob, redeemer and sufferer, seducer and victim. Whether the interaction is private or public, it is always disproportionate; the audience demand exceeds the performer's ability, and the actor is first distorted by the strain and then destroyed by it. The audience is left cheated, unappeased, unfulfilled. Love affairs and religious missions therefore share a common doom. Politically, the dissatisfied audience becomes a mob eager for violence and ripe for fascism.

West's actors are, like the artists of *Balso Snell*, fringe performers. They bear the same relation to the economy of the theater that marginal salesmen and merchants do to the economy of capitalism. The myth of success only emphasizes the reality of their failure. It lures them but always eludes them, until they become caricatures of the dream they follow. They are, that is, representative of that class of near failures which any dream spawns—tank-town performers, minor-league ballplayers, third-rate painters, businessmen who never get rich. Harry Greener's one moment of triumph—as described in the clipping he shows Tod—is itself a revelation of pain and failure. And it contains an important allusion. Though the clipping may seem, to the current reader, an implausible newspaper review of a vaudeville performance, it is done exactly in the manner of Gilbert Seldes. The blow-by-blow account of slapstick movies and vaudeville acts—with interpretative commentary—was a Seldes specialty. Compare, for example, this passage from Seldes' description of the famous Fratellini clowns with the review of Harry Greener.

[Seldes] The Fratellini, armed with a huge black box and a cloth, ask him to sit for his photograph. Francesco takes it upon himself to explain the apparatus, Paolo standing close by with the three fence posts which represent the tripod, and Alberto, the grotesque, waiting nearby. Suddenly the tripod falls on Alberto's feet and he howls with pain; Paolo picks the posts up again, and again they fall, and again he howls. It is unbelievable that this should be funny, yet it is funny beyond any capacity to describe it for one reason which the spectator senses long before he sees it. That is that the tripod is not intentionally thrown on the feet of the grotesque. The fault is Francesco's, for he is explaining the machine and making serious errors, and every time he makes a mistake Paolo gets excited and forgets that he has the tripod in his hand and simply lets it drop. One senses his acute regret, and at the next moment one realizes that his scientific zeal, his respect for his profession of photographer, simply does not permit him to let a misstatement pass; his gesture as he turns to set the matter right is so eager, so agonized, that one doesn't see what has happened to the tripod until it has fallen. And to point the moral of the matter, when the grotesque Alberto after the fifth time picks the tripod up and attempts to slay Paolo, Paolo is again turning toward the others and the blow goes wide.[4]

[West] "When Mr. Greener enters the trumpets are properly silent. Mama Ling is spinning a plate on the end of a stick held in her mouth, Papa Ling is doing cartwheels, Sister Ling is juggling fans and Sonny Ling is hanging from the proscenium arch by his pigtail. As he inspects his strenuous colleagues, Mr. Greener tries to hide his confusion under some much too obvious worldliness. He ventures to tickle Sister and receives a powerful kick in the belly in return for this innocent attention. Having been kicked, he is on familiar ground and begins to tell a dull joke. Father Ling sneaks up behind him and tosses him to Brother, who looks the other way. Mr. Greener lands on the back of his neck. He shows his mettle by finishing his dull story from a recumbent position. When he stands up, the audience, which failed to laugh at his joke, laughs at his limp, so he continues lame for the rest of the act.

Mr. Greener begins another story, even longer and duller than his first. Just before he arrives at the gag line, the orchestra blares loudly and drowns him out. He is very patient and very brave. He begins again, but the orchestra will not let him finish. The pain that almost, not quite, thank God, crumples his stiff little figure would be unbearable if it were not obviously make-believe. It is gloriously funny." (Pp. 25–26.)

Once more, West has employed parody to make a point. The contrast between the Fratellini, who were as celebrated in the twenties as Picasso or Charlie Chaplin, and Harry Greener, whose greatest moment was an appearance

[4] Seldes, pp. 302–3.

in Brooklyn with the Flying Lings, is the contrast between spectacular triumph and habitual failure. The contrast also implies a sharp dissent from Seldes' view of clowning itself. To Seldes, popular art was the modern home of the Dionysian mysteries. Slapstick was vital, joyous, possessed by the spirit of Pan, and it somehow managed to embody that other catch phrase of the twenties—irony and pity—as well.[5] To West, the clown's pain is convincing but his vitality isn't. The performance is dreary and depressing, not joyous. It carves its traces in the clown's face.

> Harry, like many actors, had very little back or top to his head. It was almost all face, like a mask, with deep furrows between the eyes, across the forehead and on either side of the nose and mouth, plowed there by years of broad grinning and heavy frowning. Because of them, he could never express anything either subtly or exactly. . . .
>
> Tod began to wonder if it might not be true that actors suffer less than other people. He thought about it for a while, then decided that he was wrong. Feeling is of the heart and nerves and the crudeness of its expression has nothing to do with its intensity. Harry suffered as keenly

[5] Seldes specifically compares Fanny Brice, Al Jolson, and Krazy Kat to Pan, and finds the same quality of "possession" [in] "religious mania, in good jazz bands, in a rare outbreak of mob violence." Seldes, pp. 191 and 238. Further, "what makes Chaplin great is that he has irony and pity," and "Mr. Herriman, who is a great ironist, understands pity." Seldes, pp. 15 and 237. The fundamental optimism of Seldes' view of American life is illustrated in his remarks on satire. "Satire is proper to America because essentially the satirist believes that life is all right, and that only the extravagances and frailties of American life, at the moment of writing, need correction or are subject to mockery." Seldes, p. 119. During the depression, Seldes' pronouncements on American life were less sanguine. He was an editor of the caustic and short-lived *Americana* (with which West was briefly associated), and in 1932 he published a study of depression America whose title, interestingly enough, was *The Year of the Locust*.

as anyone, despite the theatricality of his groans and grimaces. (P. 80.)

Like the banal masks worn by all the characters in *Miss Lonelyhearts*, Harry's mask robs him of dignity and the capacity for human expression without diminishing his capacity for human suffering.

The use of masks inevitably suggests Greek drama. As I have already said, West's mythic figures, ritual violence, and compressed, formal rhetoric probably owe a general debt to the Greek theater. *The Day of the Locust*, however, seems particularly Euripidean. Its frenzied, destructive mob recalls the fury of the bacchantes in *The Bacchae*, and Tod's vision of the Burning of Los Angeles is, like the burning torches about to fire the palace in *Orestes*, a pageant of violence, a culminating revelation of the destructive forces implicit in the drama's action. The Euripidean sense of disproportion is everywhere in West. It is not just a familiar irony—the contrast between an exalted tradition and the trivial character of an actual hero; rather, it is the contrast between the triviality of a character and the enormous power latent even in such a trivial character's actions. The drama which a Helen launches may be as petty as any suburban scandal, but it is quite capable of destroying the world. Trivial characters are possessed by demonic forces. The mythic roles they assume define the nature of the forces, and the triviality of their own characters merely reveal their powerlessness to control the forces or escape them. Riot and destruction are the natural consequences.

Song and Dance

The set speeches and confessions of *Miss Lonelyhearts* are, in *The Day of the Locust*, largely replaced by songs. They are of two kinds: the actual songs, which combine grotesque unsuitability to the singer or the scene with a curious appropriateness to both; and the background music of birds. The birds are intimately related to Faye. At Earle's and Miguel's camp, they sing a prelude to the musical scene between Faye and Miguel.

> A mocking bird was singing near by. Its song was like pebbles being dropped one by one from a height into a pool of water. Then a quail began to call, using two soft guttural notes. Another quail answered and the birds talked back and forth. Their call was not like the cheerful whistle of the Eastern bobwhite. It was full of melancholy and weariness, yet marvelously sweet. Still another quail joined the duet. This one called from near the center of the field. It was a trapped bird, but the sound it made had no anxiety in it, only sadness, impersonal and without hope. (Pp. 73–74.)

After the fight and Faye's escape, Tod lies where he has fallen on the path and hears another bird. "At first the low rich music sounded like water dripping on something hollow, the bottom of a silver pot perhaps, then like a stick dragged slowly over the strings of a harp" (p. 78). In his later fantasy of raping Faye, Tod imagines "lurking in the dark in a vacant lot, waiting for her. Whatever that bird was that sang at night in California would be bursting its heart in theatrical runs and quavers and the chill night air would smell of spice pink." (P. 152.) Faye herself is "egg-like" in her "self-sufficiency" (p. 63); and in imagining her flight from the mob in his painting, Tod thinks of her as "enjoying the release that wild flight gives in much the same way that a game bird must when, after hiding for several tense minutes, it bursts from cover in complete unthinking panic" (p. 65).

The human songs are as ritually expressive as the bird calls. Even Harry Greener's horrible laugh is thoroughly scored down to the last "metallic crackle," "obscene chuckle," and "machinelike screech" (p. 50). Faye can oppose it only by singing "Jeepers Creepers," a performance "he hated as much as she hated his laughter" (p. 49). The scene between them is simultaneously theatrical and subhuman—as unpleasant as gull screams, as deadly as any Darwinian struggle, as rehearsed and formal as an opera. With Miguel, Faye shifts from the ritual of combat to the ritual of mating.

> His voice was a plaintive tenor and it turned the revolutionary song into a sentimental lament, sweet and cloying. Faye joined in when he began another stanza. She didn't know the words, but she was able to carry the melody and to harmonize. . . .
> Their voices touched in the thin, still air to form a minor chord and it was as though their bodies had touched. (P. 75.)

At Harry Greener's funeral, the Bach chorale sounds its invitation to the Saviour politely, then with urgent pleading, then with the triumphant freedom of a bird which needs no response to its song. " 'Come or don't come,' the music seemed to say, 'I love you and my love is enough' " (p. 93). In a chapel with "imitation stained-glass windows" and "fake oak-paneled walls" (p. 92), a chapel filled with muttering, sensation-seeking spectators and a corpse so plucked and rouged that he looks "like the interlocutor in a minstrel show" (p. 88), the chorale's triumphant beauty has the strangeness of a pastoral serenade sung at a carnival. An equal strangeness pervades the other songs. A child pulling "a small sailboat on wheels" (p. 106) sings "Mama doan want no gin" with suggestive gestures, imitating "the broken groan of the blues singer quite expertly" (p. 107). A female impersonator tenderly croons a lullaby in a nightclub (p. 114). At the party which follows the cockfight, Faye sings her "Viper" song in a "lugubrious" tone, "wailing the tune as though it were a dirge" (pp. 134–35). Faye's "reedy wail" is, of course, far more suggestive of depravity and abandonment than the marihuana paradise the song describes. Like Miguel's "sweet and cloying" version of the revolutionary song, it turns sadness into a sensual wallow. It also caricatures the classic "woman wailing for her demon lover." Yet it reinforces the note of pain which is in nearly all the songs, and it defines, unmistakably, that union of sex and dream which is Faye's real lure. Her abandonment is an abandonment to fantasy. The "Viper" image—supplied ready-made by popular culture—neatly summarizes both the artificiality of the dream and its poisonous fatality.[6]

Just as the set speeches of *Miss Lonelyhearts* were accompanied by hieroglyphic images, the formal songs of *The Day of the Locust* are accompanied by ritual dances. Faye's movements are constantly choreographed. "This elaborate gesture, like all her others, was so completely meaningless, almost formal, that she seemed a dancer rather than an affected actress" (p. 47). Her dance with Miguel at the camp is as formal as any mating rite.

> They approached each other with short mincing steps. She held her skirt up and out with her thumbs and forefingers and he did the same with his trousers. . . . While

[6] "Viper" was, of course, a colloquial term for a marihuana user, and Faye's song was a real song. The only version of it I recall hearing is on an old record (*The Viper Drag*) by Fats Waller, a performance which treats the song with Waller's characteristic mock seriousness.

Faye shook her breasts and her head, holding the rest of
her body rigid, he struck the soft ground heavily with his
feet and circled her. They faced each other again and
made believe they were cradling their behinds in a shawl.
(Pp. 76–77.)

Earle attempts to invade the ritual with a "crude hoe-
down" expressive of his own role.

But he couldn't become part of their dance. Its rhythm
was like a smooth glass wall between him and the dancers.
No matter how loudly he whooped or threw himself
around, he was unable to disturb the precision with which
they retreated and advanced, separated and came together.
(P. 77.)

Earle's failure leaves him only the alternative of ritual violence—he clubs Miguel with a piece of firewood.

At the final party, Faye's monologue about herself is far
less important than her expressive movements.

None of them really heard her. They were all too busy
watching her smile, laugh, shiver, whisper, grow indig-
nant, cross and uncross her legs, stick out her tongue,
widen and narrow her eyes, toss her head so that her
platinum hair splashed against the red plush of the chair
back. The strange thing about her gestures and expressions
was that they didn't really illustrate what she was saying.
They were almost pure. It was as though her body recognized how foolish her words were and tried to excite her
hearers into being uncritical. (P. 13.)

The party careens toward violence in a series of dances—
Faye and Miguel swaying "together in long spirals that
broke rhythmically at the top of each curve into a dip" (p.
137); then Faye and Earle "stumbling" around the room in
an awkward "bear hug"; then Abe's intrusion (" 'Le'me

dance,' he barked") which ends in the fight with Earle (p. 138).

Choreography is not limited to Faye. Harry's performance for Homer is a dance composed of his entire repertoire of comic pantomime. Homer's hands, with their elaborately patterned gestures executed with "horrible . . . precision," are like dancers with a life and will of their own. "It wasn't pantomime, as [Tod] had first thought, but manual ballet" (p. 134). The dance metaphor is so omnipresent and descriptive that Tod automatically applies it to his lithographs of Abe, Harry, and Faye. And the cock fight, with its ritual passes like those in a dance, fixes the metaphor in an image whose significance extends throughout the novel.

Both song and dance are ritual performances, and both suggest at once theatrical artificiality and instinctive animality. In *The Day of the Locust*, human behavior is controlled by a double set of ceremonial patterns: the stereotypes of bad art, and the rituals of nature. Its human beings therefore seem alternately—often simultaneously —artificial and subhuman, more like birds and ballerinas than like people. The strangeness in the songs of *The Day of the Locust* derives in part from the fusion of artificial and natural ceremonies. When Miguel turns a revolutionary song into "a sentimental lament, sweet and cloying" (p. 75), or when Faye wails her "Viper" song as if it were a dirge, one cliché is being sung in the tones appropriate to another. The words are treated by the performer as meaningless in themselves. Like ceremonial phrases, they are vessels into which one pours an expressive meaning, a meaning revealed by gesture and tone of voice. The "meaning" is therefore essentially wordless. Its true expression is in bird songs and cock fights, in impulses toward mating or combat ritualized at a level below speech. Yet the words remain meaningful despite the performer's unconsciousness of them. Faye's "Viper" song is far more appropriate than she knows, and the female impersonator's lullaby is an involuntary revelation. Though the impulse may be animal in its simplicity, it is expressed in a human context where human values define its meaning, even if they cannot control its expression. And the animal impulse is also warped by the frauds and illusions of a collapsing civilization. It therefore combines cruelty with deceit, primitivism with decadence, real pains with illusory satisfactions.

The rituals of song and dance assume different meanings as they are rehearsed by different characters. To Faye and Miguel, words, like all other human attributes, are irrelevant. Pure sound and pure movement are their natural language, and they are at home in it. Homer, however, has lost animal expression without attaining speech. His hands reveal the dissociation of his personality. They dance their ritual of desire by themselves, and Homer can neither curb them nor join in their dance. He suffers constant peripheral torment and central inertness. He is sterile, sleep-ridden, "a poorly made automaton" (p. 31), both dead and disordered. And he has no words even for his anguish. Alone in his empty house, he "tries to fill it by singing" (p. 57), but "The Star-Spangled Banner" is the only song he knows. The song is ludicrously inappropriate to his mood, but unlike Faye and Miguel he cannot impose his mood upon it. His song expresses nothing but futility.

The Dandy and the Bitch

> Love's claws, and that sharp poison which is sin,
> Are dulled against the granite of her skin.

Death she defies, Debauch she smiles upon,
For their sharp scythe-like talons every one
Pass by her in their all-destructive play;
Leaving her beauty till a later day . . .
She knows, and she believes, this sterile maid
Without whom the world's onward dream would fade,
That bodily beauty is the supreme gift
Which may from every sin the terror lift.
Hell she ignores, and Purgatory defies;
And when black Night shall roll before her eyes,
She will look straight in Death's grim face forlorn,
Without remorse or hate—as one newborn.
            —Baudelaire, "Allégorie"[7]

She was now revealed in a sense as the symbolic incarnation of world-old Vice, the goddess of immortal Hysteria, the Curse of Beauty supreme above all other beauties by the cataleptic spasm that stirs her flesh and steels her muscles,—a monstrous Beast of the Apocalypse, indifferent, irresponsible, poisoning, like Helen of Troy of the old Classic fables, all who come near her, all who see her, all who touch her.—Huysmans[8]

Baudelaire and Huysmans are hardly the only writers to have been fascinated by the immortal whore, but their portraits of her bear some distinctive features. They also bear more than a casual resemblance to Faye Greener. Like the woman of Baudelaire's "Allegorie," Faye is herself impervious to the destruction she spreads. Her beauty is "structural like a tree's, not a quality of her mind or heart." Perhaps even whoring couldn't damage it for that reason,

[7] Baudelaire, "Allégorie," *Fleurs du Mal: A Selection*, ed. Marthiel and Jackson Mathews (New York: New Directions Paperbooks, 1955), p. 123. The translation of this particular poem is by F. P. Sturm. Reprinted by permission of New Directions Publishing Corporation and Jackson Mathews. Copyright © 1955, 1962 by New Directions.
[8] Huysmans, *Against the Grain*, p. 145.

only age or accident or disease." (P. 89.) And whoring doesn't. Even after she has been a call girl, been involved with both Earle and Miguel, and settled into her parasitic life at Homer's expense, she still looks "just born, everything moist and fresh, volatile and perfumed" (p. 108).[9] At the novel's end, she simply disappears. Though Homer has already been destroyed and the final riot is imminent, Tod is sure of her curious invulnerability. "Nothing could hurt her. She was like a cork. No matter how rough the sea got, she would go dancing over the same waves that sank iron ships and tore away piers of reinforced concrete." (P. 151.)

Faye eludes unwanted embraces as easily as she eludes destruction. To most of those who desire her, she is therefore just a phantom, "fatally suggestive [to] the imaginations that she haunts and fertilizes."[10] The phrase is Baudelaire's, and it defines a second major theme in the Symbolist-Decadent treatment of the Bitch: her dream function, especially her effect upon imaginations already addicted to fantasy and bored or frustrated by actuality. To Huysmans, the Bitch's dream presence is more real and more fatal than her actual presence, so much so that the woman who torments Durtal in *Là Bas* is nearly—perhaps even literally—a succubus. And in his comments on Félicien Rops, Huysmans praised Rops' portrayal of the "Spirit of Lust, of isolated erotic ideas without material correspondences," of the "impulse toward a preternatural debauchery, a plea for those convulsions which elude the flesh." This "livid impulsion," says Huysmans, is called by science "mental hysteria" and by the Church a "morose delectation"; it is the enjoyment of evil in the imagination. As in the fantasies of Sade, the imagination becomes monstrous in

---

[9] Stanley Edgar Hyman has made the same point. See Hyman, p. 34.
[10] Baudelaire, *Prose and Poetry*, p. 235.

proportion to the impotence of the flesh, until at last "the natural act is effaced, as denuded of interest, as too brief, as provoking only a too well known commotion, a cry of banality. . . ."[11] The combination of jaded senses and fevered imagination described here is of course the familiar condition of the decadent hero. It is also exactly the condition of the shadowy spectators in *The Day of the Locust*, those lower middle-class fanatics who impress Tod with the "contrast between their drained-out feeble bodies and their wild, disordered minds" (p. 109). Like the dandy, they have lost even the capacity for fulfillment in the ordinary world. The newspapers and movies have "fed them on lynchings, murders, sex crimes, explosions, wrecks, love nests, fires, miracles, revolutions, wars. This daily diet made sophisticates of them. The sun is a joke. Oranges can't titillate their jaded palates. Nothing can ever be violent enough to make taut their slack minds and bodies." (P. 157.)

The dandy's love of artifice is as omnipresent as his thwarted fantasies and latent violence. The Huysmansesque decor of Wu Fong's whorehouse reappears in Claude Estee's home, "an exact reproduction of the old Dupuy mansion near Biloxi, Mississippi" (p. 13), complete with boxwood hedges and a two-story porch with a wicker swing. As an added novelty, his swimming pool contains a dead horse made of rubber. Homer's house

> had an enormous and very crooked stone chimney, little dormer windows with big hoods and a thatched roof that came down very low on both sides of the front door. This door was of gumwood painted like fumed oak and it hung on enormous hinges. Although made by machine, the hinges had been carefully stamped to appear hand-forged.

[11] Huysmans, *Down Stream and Other Works,* trans. Samuel Putnam, pp. 284–86.

The same kind of care and skill had been used to make the roof thatching, which was not really straw but heavy fireproof paper colored and ribbed to look like straw.

The prevailing taste had been followed in the living room. It was "Spanish." The walls were pale orange flecked with pink and on them hung several silk armorial banners in red and gold. A big galleon stood on the mantelpiece. Its hull was plaster, its sails paper and its rigging wire. In the fireplace was a variety of cactus in gaily colored Mexican pots. Some of the plants were made of rubber and cork; others were real. . . .

In the two small bedrooms still another style had been used. This the agent had called "New England." There was a spool bed made of iron grained like wood, a Windsor chair of the kind frequently seen in tea shops, and a Governor Winthrop dresser painted to look like unpainted pine. (Pp. 29–30.)

And of course Tod muses on all the "Mexican ranch houses, Samoan huts, Mediterranean villas, Egyptian and Japanese temples, Swiss chalets, Tudor cottages" (p. 3) which line the hills of Hollywood.

On the corner of La Huerta Road was a miniature Rhine castle with tarpaper turrets pierced for archers. Next to it was a little highly colored shack with domes and minarets out of the *Arabian Nights*. Again he was charitable. Both houses were comic, but he didn't laugh. Their desire to startle was so eager and guileless.

It is hard to laugh at the need for beauty and romance, no matter how tasteless, even horrible, the results of that need are. But it is easy to sigh. Few things are sadder than the truly monstrous. (P. 4.)

The "truly monstrous" is perhaps a natural result of that "burning need for individuality"[12] which, according to Baudelaire, underlies the dandy's pose.

[12] Baudelaire, quoted in Pia, p. 67.

Fixation upon dream figures is equally natural. Where Miss Lonelyhearts was an ersatz Christ, Faye is a debased Venus, a transient focus of eternal desire. Her appeal is universal. She attracts Tod and Homer and Claude Estee and Earle and Miguel and Abe Kusich, and she is also the naked girl who flees the mob in Tod's painting, the principal object of revenge for all those whose dreams have embittered and betrayed them. She is at once the natural object of sexual desire and the object of a desire hopelessly perverted by fantasies. She embodies the fatal power of all illusions, inflaming and degrading desire without ever satisfying it. When Tod tells Homer, " 'She's a whore!' " (p. 136), his condemnation extends to all those dreams which Faye represents.[13]

To discover the falseness of an illusion is not, however, to be delivered from it. Insight may only intensify frustration. The lurid colors of fantasy make reality pale and insufficient, and those who have become addicted to dreams of "lynchings, murders, sex crimes"—or to "convulsions which elude the flesh"—can only regard the actual world with "an expression of vicious, acrid boredom that tremble [s] on the edge of violence" (p. 91). The psychology of decadence may be fascinating when it is novel or when it can be confused with sensitivity. When it becomes a mass phenomenon, however, when the streets are full of dandies with cheap, mail-order clothing and manufactured dreams, violence is ominously real.

Another aspect of the Bitch's appeal is perhaps even more important than her falseness. To Baudelaire, "all sensual

---

[13] James Light has made substantially the same point. See Light, pp. 160–61.

delights stem from evil,"[14] and to Huysmans, woman is "the nude and poisonous Beast, the Mercenary of Darkness."[15] These attitudes cannot be transferred to West without important qualification. He has none of Baudelaire's voluptuous response to sensual evil and none of that peculiar nastiness which often pervades Huysmans' disgust—a disgust which led him to see in Degas' female nudes "the humid horror inspired by a body which no lotion can purify."[16] West's visions of sexuality in *The Day of the Locust* often inspire horror, but it is a horror of pain, not a "humid" revulsion from uncleanness. Yet West owes a debt to Huysmans. Consider, for example, this passage from one of Huysmans' discussions of erotic art.

> With the Japanese, carnal commerce appears to disrupt the nervous system. . . . It tortures the couples who indulge in it, shriveling their fists and contorting their quivering legs, while the very toes of their feet writhe in anguish.
>
> Their women, with indolent flesh, white as emphysemas, agonize upon their backs, their eyes closed, their teeth clenched in the blood of their lips. Their bellies, frightfully split, yawn like a caruncular wound, while the men, in death-throes upon their backs, rear inconceivable phalli, terminating in parasols, with tubular swellings and trenched with veins. Tangled in impossible poses, they all lie like cadavers whose bones have been broken by powerful strappadoes.[17]

The sadistic tones of this rhetoric echo in *The Day of the Locust*. Where sex was in *Balso Snell* a disguised motive for

---

[14] Baudelaire, *Fusées*, quoted in Pia, p. 61.
[15] Huysmans, *Down Stream* . . . , p. 315.
[16] *Ibid.*, p. 280.
[17] *Ibid.*, pp. 290–91.

arty imposture and in *Miss Lonelyhearts* a symbol of the misery inherent in nature, it is in this novel specifically associated with cruelty and torture. Faye herself is described by Tod in terms of fascinated horror.

Her invitation wasn't to pleasure, but to struggle, hard and sharp, closer to murder than to love. If you threw yourself on her, it would be like throwing yourself from the parapet of a skyscraper. You would do it with a scream. You couldn't expect to rise again. Your teeth would be driven back into your skull like nails into a pine board and your back would be broken. You wouldn't even have time to sweat or close your eyes. (P. 12.)

Little Adore's precocious song ends with his voice carrying a "top-heavy load of sexual pain" (p. 108). Homer, in a mistake which reveals more than his naïveté, interprets Faye's moans as the sounds of extreme agony and is shocked to find her in bed with Miguel. (P. 146.) Earle Shoop, one of Faye's paramours, habitually stands in front of the saddlery store whose windows contain, "a large collection of torture instruments . . . fancy braided quirts, spurs with great spiked wheels and double bits that looked as though they could break a horse's jaw without any trouble" (p. 65). The hen which so horrifies Homer is a peculiarly vivid example. "The roosters have torn all the feathers off its neck and made its comb all bloody and it has scabby feet covered with warts and it cackles so nasty when they put it into the pen" (p. 116). Miguel likes to drop the hen in with the roosters just for fun, and it adds to his fun to make Homer watch. Significantly, Faye does not object, saying, "It's only natural" (p. 117).

It isn't *only* natural, of course, but it is entirely appropriate to Faye and to that mixture of natural and perverse desire which she represents. The two scenes in which both Faye herself and the men around her become most aroused follow immediately upon images of cruelty. The first is at Earle and Miguel's camp.

> Earle caught the birds one at a time and pulled their heads off. . . .
> He gutted the birds, then began cutting them into quarters with a pair of heavy tin shears. Faye held her hands over her ears in order not to hear the soft click made by the blades as they cut through flesh and bone. . . .
> For all her squeamishness, Faye ate as heartily as the men did. . . .
> Tod could sense her growing excitement. . . . He could feel how hot she was and how restless. . . . (Pp. 74–75.)

This excitement leads to Faye's explicitly sexual dance with Miguel, then to the fight between Miguel and Earle, followed by Faye's escape as Tod pursues her with the single intention of rape. The second scene, of course, is that which follows the cockfight. Faye's effect on the men is then more dramatic than it has ever been, and she is herself more abandoned than ever before. It is here that Faye finally becomes the full dream goddess. Her bits of make-believe drama and fan-magazine legend become, mixed with the "almost pure" gestures of her body, suddenly real, suddenly completely compelling. "It worked that night; no one even thought of laughing at her. The only move they made was to narrow their circle about her." (P. 131.) This apotheosis, in which the consummation of cruelty and sexuality transforms Faye into the dream figure she has always wanted to be, again has a parallel in *Miss Lonelyhearts*. Just as Miss Lonelyhearts' achievement of a

final state of complete religious hysteria precipitates both
his own death and Doyle's disaster, so Faye's transforma-
tion precipitates Homer's ruin and, thereby, the mob violence which almost literally fulfills Tod's vision of the
Burning of Los Angeles. When Faye, the whore of everybody's dreams, succeeds in totally destroying Homer, the
fury of all the cheated dreamers is unleashed. The mob
riots, threatening to destroy everyone and everything except Faye herself.

From Winesburg, Ohio, to the Promised Land

From the story "Queer," it is possible to abstract the
choreography of *Winesburg*. Its typical action is a series
of dance maneuvers by figures whose sole distinctive characteristic is an extreme deformity of movement or posture.
Each of these grotesques dances, with angular indirection
and muted pathos, toward a central figure who seems to
them young, fresh, and radiant.—Irving Howe.[18]

The choreography of *Winesburg, Ohio* is, of course,
the choreography of both *Miss Lonelyhearts* and *The Day
of the Locust*. The role of central figure is enacted first by
Miss Lonelyhearts and then by Faye Greener, and the
grotesques "whose sole distinctive characteristic is an extreme deformity of movement or posture" are omnipresent
in both novels. Even the letters and confessions which
Miss Lonelyhearts receives illustrate a choreographic
pattern—they are like figures who briefly detach themselves
from a crowd and dance to the center of the stage, then
retreat back into the anonymous mass which fills the wings
and overbalances the central action. The pathos of their

[18] Irving Howe, *Sherwood Anderson*, American Men of Letters Series,
p. 105.

gestures is no longer "muted," but the dances are as angular, imploring, and ineffectual as any in Anderson.

West's debt to Anderson is not, however, confined to the choreographic pattern of thwarted grotesques reaching toward a "radiant" figure. Echoes of Anderson are everywhere in West's two best novels, and in *The Day of the Locust* they are so explicit that he must have intended his readers to notice them, perhaps even to regard them as a variation upon—almost a sequel to—the themes of *Winesburg, Ohio*. Homer's hands are, of course, taken directly from Wing Biddlebaum, the grotesque whose "slender expressive fingers, forever active, forever striving to conceal themselves in his pockets or behind his back"[19] become, in *Winesburg, Ohio*, the perfect symbol of that baffled and wordless urge for expression which forces each character into the "extreme deformity" of his dance. The identification is underscored by the town from which Homer comes—Wayneville, Iowa, is surely a deliberate echo of Winesburg, Ohio. And the identification is as complicated and thorough as it is deliberate. The hands are not just the picturesque attribute of a single grotesque; rather, they embody a theory of the grotesque itself—they reduce a

[19] *Winesburg, Ohio*, p. 5. Both the specific connection between Homer and Wing Biddlebaum and the general resemblance between West and Anderson was briefly noted by Daniel Aaron in 1951. Aaron says that Homer "is nothing more than a botched reworking of Sherwood Anderson's grotesque in his story, *Hands*," and that West's "obsession with the grotesque, his studies of people suddenly seized and ridden by private demons, suggest Sherwood Anderson." See Aaron, "Waiting for the Apocalypse," pp. 634–36. I do not agree that the reworking is "botched" and I think Aaron misses the point of the identification with *Winesburg*, but his remarks are perceptive. John Sanford's reminiscences established that West had read Anderson by the late twenties. See Light, p. 63.

complete psychology to an image. The psychology could be summarized in two prevailing laws: the first is the familiar "I can't express it"; the second is "I can't *not* express it, either." The interaction of these two laws inevitably twists human beings into grotesques. Anderson's people are wordless and compulsive, as unable to control or understand their desires as they are to express them. Their desperation escapes in exaggerated but ineffectual gestures: a bartender who cannot find words to ask a girl to marry him threatens her with violence instead; a girl who is too shy even to speak to a man puts a note under his door offering to give herself to him; a mother who gets up from her death bed to stalk her husband with a pair of scissors can manage no expression of love for the son she wanted to save. These dramatic acts are—like the mute gestures of Biddlebaum's hands—revelations of that for which the characters have no words.

But, though the acts are revealing, they are always distorted and ineffectual—or grotesque. Anderson's characters manage neither to say nor to do what they mean. Their vocabulary of actions is as crude and limited as their speech. And they are further inhibited by fears, misunderstandings, accidents, and accurate insights—by that complex of barriers, real and imagined, which deflects the intensity of their desire into despondency and irrelevant agitation. *Winesburg, Ohio* is a succession of thwarted climaxes. Its characters all approach the moment of release—defined as expressive communion with someone else—only to be driven back from it. Wing Biddlebaum is suddenly alarmed by the caressing motions of his hands and hurries away from George Willard; Elizabeth Willard and Doctor Reefy are startled from their embrace by the sound of a clerk's footsteps on the stairs; Alice Hindman, escaping from loneliness into hysterical abandon, calls to an old man whose incomprehending response jolts her into shamed and frightened retreat. The sexual implications of these incidents are both insistent and ambiguous. It seems equally true that the expressive urge is really a sexual urge and that the sexual urge is just a particular form of the expressive urge. The ambiguity is the same as that expressed by Faulkner's Benjy, whose own version of his assault on a female child is "I was trying to say."

In *The Day of the Locust*, the psychology of baffled expression is both elaborated and intensified. Homer is, even more than Wing Biddlebaum, a type figure, one who represents in extreme form the predicament of all those whose desire is inarticulate but inextinguishable. He is afflicted by a characteristic emotional impotence.

> His emotions surged up in an enormous wave, curving and rearing, higher and higher, until it seemed as though the wave must carry everything before it. But the crash never came. Something always happened at the very top of the crest and the wave collapsed to run back like water down a drain, leaving, at the most, only the refuse of feeling. (P. 37.)

Sleep is the element Homer lives in. It is the only element he can live in, for consciousness means hopeless pain. For Homer, there is no release, no purgation, no catharsis.

> Only those who still have hope can benefit from tears. When they finish they feel better. But to those without hope, like Homer, whose anguish is basic and permanent, no good comes from crying. Nothing changes for them. They usually know this, but still can't help crying. (P. 58.)

Homer is at peace only when he is without sensation, when he can sit mindlessly in his yard day after day watching a lizard hunt flies. "Whether he was happy or not it is hard to say. Probably he was neither, just as a plant is neither." (P. 41.) But Homer is vulnerable in a way that plants are not. His hands, which are so estranged from him that he fumbles "with the buttons of his clothing as though he were undressing a stranger" (p. 31), are alive and responsive, and they betray him. In Faye's presence, not even cold showers can subdue them.

> His hands began to bother him. He rubbed them against the edge of the table to relieve their itch, but it only stimulated them. When he clasped them behind his back, the strain became intolerable. They were hot and swollen. Using the dishes as an excuse, he held them under the cold water tap of the sink. (P. 53.)

Faye awakens Homer's desire and fixes it in an object—herself—which is unattainable and therefore destructive. Homer's desire does not unify him; instead, it merely increases the agitation of his dislocated consciousness. It gives him an object to strain toward without the coherence of feeling which would make release possible. Sexual awareness is itself fatal. "He somehow knew that his only defense was chastity, that it served him, like the shell of a tortoise, as both spine and armor. He couldn't shed it even in thought. If he did, he would be destroyed." (P. 56.) And the destruction will not be limited to Homer himself. When desire has no real expression, it can only escape in violence. Homer, the man "incapable of hatred" (p. 116), ends in a brutal assault on Adore which releases the latent fury of the crowd.

In both Anderson and West, the grotesque is normal. Its

crippled or violent gestures are the visible symptoms of primitive urgency straining toward expression. Primitivism, like decadence, is controlled by the psychology of unremitting stimulus and thwarted response. It differs from decadence in that it has not yet attained speech, while decadence has exhausted it and returned to a wordless condition. The exhaustion of decadence is often literal; its violence may be entirely of the mind, without physical consequence—at least until its apocalyptic fantasies find an opportunity to become real. But the primitive character is unable even to think his desires. Action is his only language, and his exaggerated motions are, like the mute's proverbial violence, gestures expressive of his condition. Anderson's grotesque primitives are not, of course, animalistic. Like Homer, they have lost instinctive ease without having attained speech. They therefore reach in two directions: toward the wilderness from which they have emerged, and toward the shining city which they have not yet found. The fecundity of nature stimulates and mocks them; their lives are thwarted, but Eden seems all around them, if they could just get back in. Or the Promised Land beckons somewhere in the distance—a world of glamour, romance, and richer life. It dominates the dreams of Elizabeth Willard for her son and of Alice Hindman for her lover.

The citizens of *Winesburg, Ohio* are, in other words, a lost tribe. They are alien from their surroundings, yearning for a lost past or a promised future which will end their exile and fulfill their dreams. In *The Day of the Locust*, they have found it. The lost tribe has, a generation later, left its Midwestern towns and arrived in the Promised Land. But the Promised Land is only southern California, a world "of sunshine and oranges" where "nothing happens"

(p. 156). It is a dead end. The continent has been crossed, there is nowhere left to go, there is nothing to do but stand on the shore and stare at the waves. Inarticulate seeking yields to vicious boredom.

> All their lives they had slaved at some kind of dull, heavy labor, behind desks and counters, in the fields and at tedious machines of all sorts, saving their pennies and dreaming of the leisure that would be theirs when they had enough. Finally that day came. . . . Where else should they go but California, the land of sunshine and oranges?
>
> Once there, they discover that sunshine isn't enough. . . . They haven't the mental equipment for leisure, the money nor the physical equipment for pleasure. Did they slave so long just to go to an occasional Iowa picnic? What else is there? If only a plane would crash once in a while so that they could watch the passengers being consumed in a "holocaust of flame," as the newspapers put it. But the planes never crash. (Pp. 156–57.)

West's people are primitives who have suddenly inherited decadence. The dull yearning of their lives has, under a steady diet of "lynchings, murders, sex crimes," become focused upon phantoms of excitement, phantoms which have no real home. The crowd's savagery derives from this perception. They have tracked their dream to its source and found that it was only a fraud. They have nothing left to seek except revenge.

Dreams of a Promised Land or a Fabulous City are as perpetual as the hope for a Redeemer. They are perhaps as inevitable as the frustrations they seek to console. In both Anderson and West, however, eternal dreams are warped by a peculiarly American combination of cynicism and naïveté. Like the ambitious parents of Anderson's "The

Egg," West's characters read advertising as if it were prophetic scripture. They accept its definitions of their desires, and they invest their lives in its promises. But the promises are all false. The Redeemer is just a lovelorn columnist and the Promised Land is just a real-estate promotion. The lie is not, of course, the only evil. In both Anderson and West, the life force produces endless grotesques—people warped by desires which have no satisfaction or by miseries which have no cure. The specific evil of the lie is that it debases even the unhappiness of life. When focused on meretricious objects, desire itself is degraded. And the false promise is always worse than real pain. The victim discovers that he has been swindled, that he is a sucker as well as a sufferer, and that therefore his miserable life is a joke.

Both Anderson and West remain always aware of the joke. Their tone is controlled by its implications, as in this passage from Anderson's "The Untold Lie."

> He couldn't make out what was wrong. Every time he raised his eyes and saw the beauty of the country in the failing light he wanted to do something he had never done before, shout or scream or hit his wife with his fists or something equally unexpected and terrifying. Along the path he went scratching his head and trying to make it out. He looked hard at his wife's back but she seemed all right.[20]

The rueful and baffled humor here is as important as the urge toward violence. Though Anderson takes his characters seriously, he remains always aware that they are comic, even ludicrous. Yet his sense of the ludicrous never blinds him to the force which lies behind their ridiculous acts.

[20] Anderson, *Winesburg, Ohio*, p. 151.

Indeed, the ludicrous inadequacy of their acts, like that of their words, only makes the inarticulate urge more desperate. Violence is always latent in *Winesburg, Ohio*, and it is often actual. Despair, even when it is comic, is oppressively prevalent and real.

Precision of tone is responsible for the peculiar authority of both Anderson's and West's treatments of thwarted characters. They have none of the "proletarian" writer's willed identification with victims and none of the mingled condescension and sentimentality which taints so many irony-and-pity portrayals of the lower orders. Instead, the identification is involuntary, often painful. Irving Howe has described Anderson's use of the oral narrator's craft—his ability to involve his audience with "his struggle to tell his story almost as much as with the story itself," his use of "the voice of a hesitant human being" as his "controlling point of view."[21] At times, this "hesitant" voice deliberately exploits the attributes of the Rube. The narrator is both shrewd and clumsy. He tells a story whose punch line is the rueful, half-inadvertent admission that the joke is really on himself—and that the joke hurts. The grotesques in "The Egg" are as misshapen as any sideshow freaks. The story's triumph is that they are also recognizably human, even recognizably related to the narrator himself. Humor is, in these terms, far more moving than tears. It is the only response to a perception sadder than any tragedy—the grotesque is normal, but it is still grotesque.

The sense of unwilled and painful kinship produces, in Anderson's best stories, what Howe has called "the tone of love."[22] In West, the kinship is also unwilled and painful,

[21] Howe, p. 149.
[22] *Ibid.*, p. 152.

but love does not control its tone. The reflected image of
the self one sees in others is repellent. It is a kinship in
ugliness and evil, not just in suffering. Tod himself, though
both a humane and essentially non-violent man, constantly
dreams of raping Faye, of smashing her self-sufficiency
with a blow (p. 109), of clubbing her with a bottle (p.
152). He suspects that he shares "the ingrained, morbid
apathy he liked to draw in others" (p. 109), and he is aware
of the mixture of envy, hatred, and suicidal compulsion in
his attraction toward Faye. Like the crowd, he has an itch
for apocalypse, for the climactic violence of some final act.

The authority of West's portraits derives, like Anderson's, from helpless recognition. His distinctive tone is that
of the numbed but inextinguishable spectator in the self,
that spectator who hears one shout, sees one strike. It is a
tone of almost voiceless shock. The most appalling fact of
Tod's desire for Faye is that it does not blind him. He
knows what she is, but his knowledge changes nothing.
It leaves him only with the perception that Faye is shallow,
selfish, and false, and that his own deepest response is exactly to that vicious dream which she embodies. The inner
witness is as incapable of controlling the self's violence as it
is of being deceived by it. And it views the rest of the
world with the same impotent clarity.

The orchestra started and Tod was able to ignore her
question. All three of them turned to watch a young man
in a tight evening gown of red silk sing a lullaby.
> *"Little man, you're crying,*
> *I know why you're blue,*
> *Someone took your kiddycar away;*
> *Better go to sleep now,*
> *Little man, you've had a busy day . . ."*

He had a soft, throbbing voice and his gestures were

matronly, tender and aborted, a series of unconscious ca-
resses. What he was doing was in no sense parody; it was
too simple and too restrained. It wasn't even theatrical.
This dark young man with his thin, hairless arms and soft,
rounded shoulders, who rocked an imaginary cradle as he
crooned, was really a woman.

When he had finished, there was a great deal of ap-
plause. The young man shook himself and became an actor
again. He tripped on his train, as though he weren't used
to it, lifted his skirts to show he was wearing Paris garters,
then strode off swinging his shoulders. His imitation of a
man was awkward and obscene. (Pp. 114–115.)

There is nothing to be done with such a perception. It
invalidates every comfortable response, whether scorn or
pity or enlightened tolerance. No possible combination of
social acceptance and Danish surgery could really change
this "matronly" young man's fate, and no amount of sympathetic understanding will help Homer. The grotesque is
natural, but it is still grotesque.

The absence of love in West's tone can, in part, be
understood in terms of the difference between his world
and Anderson's. When decadence replaces primitivism, the
fellowship of seeking yields to the sense of mutual betrayal.
There is no longer even a visionary alternative to a
thwarted life. And submission becomes as difficult as continued dreaming. The members of West's mob have lost
that instinctive kindness which, in the father of "The Egg,"
turns away from violence and resolves frustration in a com-
ically bleak submission to despair. West's characters have
been depraved as well as cheated. They do not even want
love. They are victims, but they will revenge themselves on
other victims. Apocalyptic violence is their one remaining
dream.

The Spectator of Collapse

The Day of the Locust is often accused of lacking unity, sometimes on the ground that Tod Hackett is too much just a point of view, not a participant, in the drama which surrounds Faye. The accusation is fair in one sense and beside the point in another. Obviously, the novel lacks the linear momentum of *Miss Lonelyhearts,* and Tod's separation from the central action is one reason that it does. But, just as obviously, *The Day of the Locust* gains in range and veracity much of what it loses in tension. And the final chapters reveal, I think, a thematic unity and dramatic inevitability even more persuasive than the end of *Miss Lonelyhearts.* Tod's "separation" is again in part responsible. He is not just a device. Rather, he defines that mixture of impotence, violence, concern, and detachment which is West's distinctive literary persona.

Tod is not a non-participant through choice. His pursuit of Faye is as unceasing as it is ineffectual, and he involves himself, again unceasingly and ineffectually, in the troubles of Harry Greener and Homer. He is simply powerless, peripheral to all dramas yet implicated in their action. Like Prufrock, he is "not Prince Hamlet, nor was meant to be." But, unlike Prufrock, his helplessness is not just a personal tragedy. Nor does it relieve itself in poignant reveries about his own isolation. Tod's ineffectuality is a failure, a failure which, though it has its personal implications, takes its full meaning from the spectacle of public violence with which the novel ends.[23]

[23] Victor Comerchero has, in somewhat different terms, also discussed the 'impotence' of West's central characters and has compared Tod's function in *The Day* to that of Tiresias in Eliot's *Waste Land.* See Comerchero, pp. 125–26 and 162.

Tod is an unconvincing and clumsy actor. His only authority is the clarity of his vision, and he remains a spectator even as he acts. He is, I think, obviously modeled in part on West himself. The reminiscences of West's friends seem always to combine admiration with amusement, even with condescension. His poses as the dandy or the hunter are recalled in anecdotes which unfailingly reveal his ineptness in the role.[24] He was "everybody's kid brother,"[25] "Pep," "Tweedy Boy," an ill-coordinated, shambling figure who had trouble with "so little a thing as lighting a cigarette."[26] His illusions are remembered in the accents of fond superiority with which adults describe the make-believe of children. Obviously, he must have aroused similar responses—minus the admiration and the fondness—in those who were not his friends. West was the sort of man who is sure to be patronized, especially by his inferiors.

And even more sure to be cruelly dissected by himself. A sense of disbelief in the self's poses is everywhere in his novels. Miss Lonelyhearts cannot persuade himself—let alone others—of his role's validity, and when he tries to switch from priest to seducer, he remains unconvinced and therefore unconvincing.

"The way to be gay is to make other people gay," Miss Lonelyhearts said. "Sleep with me and I'll be one gay dog."
The defeat in his voice made it easy for her to ignore his request and her mind sagged with his. (P. 94.)

[24] See, for example, Sanford, pp. 10–13; Herbst, pp. 310–44; Hellman, p. 80; and Light, pp. 6–16, 69, 105, 131–32, and 146–47. The reminiscences do not, of course, record only West's inept moments. They also reveal his consistent kindness, his curious mixture of awkwardness and poise, and his enthusiasms for particular people and causes.
[25] Malcolm Cowley, "It's the Telling That Counts," p. 4.
[26] Sanford, pp. 11 and 13.

The same pattern is repeated in Tod's pursuit of Faye. In the nightclub, he begs her to sleep with him and receives the refusal he expected. "He was grateful to her for having behaved so well, for not having made him feel too ridiculous" (p. 113). Tod is, almost as much as Homer, the kind of man it is easy to say no to, the kind in whom a sense of decency conspires with a sense of inferiority to make dominance impossible. He is the man women like Faye inevitably choose—and use—as "friends." His unhappiness with her is only partly caused by her rejection of him as a lover. Her rejection of his vision of her is even more painful. The sense of her degradation, her indifference to every standard—aesthetic or moral—which he values, produces in Tod an agonized shock like Miss Lonelyhearts' response to mass suffering. And his attempt to express his shock is nearly as trite, hysterical, and weak as the gospel Miss Lonelyhearts preaches to the Doyles.

> He had to say something. She wouldn't understand the aesthetic argument and with what values could he back up the moral one? The economic didn't make sense either. Whoring certainly paid. Half of the customer's thirty dollars. Say ten men a week.
> She kicked at his shins, but he held on to her. Suddenly he began to talk. He had found an argument. Disease would destroy her beauty. He shouted at her like a Y.M.C.A. lecturer on sex hygiene. (Pp. 89–90.)

Tod is afflicted with a moral impulse whose traditional forms have collapsed. He is therefore an impotent but insistent moralist, just as he is an ineffectual but persistent lover. He recalls George Grosz's "Self Portrait":

> I have no program. . . . Perhaps I am something of a muddlehead and certainly with one foot a petit bourgeois.

I still believe in certain forbidden metaphysical concepts like Truth, Justice, and Humanity.[27]

In the final mob scene, Tod's impotent concern is perfectly dramatized. He first tries to protect Homer, then to stop Homer's murderous attack on Adore.

Tod yelled for him to stop and tried to yank him away. He shoved Tod and went on using his heels. Tod hit him as hard as he could, first in the belly, then in the face. He ignored the blows and continued to stamp on the boy. Tod hit him again and again, then threw both arms around him and tried to pull him off. He couldn't budge him. He was like a stone column. (Pp. 160–61.)

This failure is immediately submerged in the impotent terror of being swept up by the crowd. Tod is "jostled about in a hacking cross surf of shoulders and backs," struggling to slip "sideways against the tide," ground between opposing forces "like a grain between millstones" (p. 161). His terror is increased by "slowly being pushed into the air. Although relief for his cracking ribs could be gotten by continuing to rise, he fought to keep his feet on the ground. Not being able to touch was an even more dreadful sensation than being carried backwards." (Pp. 161–62.) The sea imagery of "surf" and "tide" and involuntary buoyancy is entirely natural to the scene. But it is also very familiar. It recalls Tod's vision of Faye as the "bright cork" whose buoyancy is triumphant. "Wave after wave reared its ton on ton of solid water and crashed down only to have her spin gaily away" (p. 151). It also recalls the imagery of *Miss Lonelyhearts*, which, in the person of Mrs. Doyle,

[27] George Grosz, "Self Portrait of the Artist," p. 22.

united "tidal, moon-driven" heaves with "massive hams" like "two enormous grindstones" (p. 106). It is an imagery which expresses the fantasy of impotence in all its forms: being engulfed, ground to pieces, swept away, borne helplessly aloft to bob at the mercy of pure force. The sexual application of these images is obvious. But it is also somewhat misleading. For one thing, the mob is a mob, not just a metaphor. Not to feel impotent in its grip would be insane. For another, the metaphor itself cannot just be reduced to a vision of awful, engulfing femininity. The feminine sea imagery is matched by the masculine flame imagery of Tod's "Burning of Los Angeles," and in the midst of the crowd's wave-like surges, an "old man, wearing a Panama hat and horn-rimmed glasses," attacks a helpless and hysterical girl. "He had one of his hands inside her dress and was biting her neck" (p. 162). Like the destructive forces in *Miss Lonelyhearts*, the mob's fury is both masculine and feminine. It is the violent release of all desire—desire so basic that the sexes are just alternate and mutually destructive forms of a single impulse. The desire combines savagery and depravity. It is an instinctive force which has been thwarted and perverted without being civilized. In Freudian terms, it is the anarchic revolt of a mass id against those "higher" powers which have denied it and tricked it. In Marxist terms, it is the outrage of victims who have been cynically exploited by a system. In Nietzschean terms, it is the revenge of Dionysian frenzy against a fraudulent Apollonian dream. The phenomenon is so fundamental that it can be understood in several descriptive languages, but the Nietzschean vocabulary is particularly appropriate. Nietzsche's famous contrast between Apollo and Dionysus was not, of course, simply a contrast between control and license. The special Apollonian mode, according to Nietzsche, was dream, just as the special Dionysian mode was intoxication. The Apollonian vision of Olympus reconciled the Greeks to existence; it was an ideal mirror of human life which first subdued the terror and pain of barbarity and then resisted, civilized, and absorbed the threat of invading Dionysian cults. Under the influence of Apollo, Dionysian worship was transformed from a "paroxysm of lust and cruelty" into "rites of universal redemption, glorious transfiguration."[28] The "treaty" between Apollo and Dionysus was a crucial step in civilization, a reconciliation, however unstable, between amoral vitality and controlled beauty. The dream therefore has a double benefit: happiness and restraint. It is a weapon against the natural condition whose passive form is unrelieved suffering (as in *Miss Lonelyhearts*) and whose active form is savage frenzy (as in *The Day of the Locust*). When dreams "have been made puerile," as Miss Lonelyhearts puts it, destruction is as inevitable as pain.

Tod is, in these terms, an impotent Apollonian. He cannot compete with Earle and Miguel in the primitive struggle, and he cannot create any alternative to it. The standards of compassion and decency which he tries to maintain are vitiated by his own disbelief in their authority. They seem irrelevant to the world which confronts him, powerless to help or control anything. They are also contradicted by the morbid and violent impulses within himself. Neither abandonment nor resistance can help. Though Tod tells Homer that he could learn from Abe Kusich (p. 133), the

[28] Friedrich Nietzsche, *The Birth of Tragedy*, quoted in Richard Ellmann and Charles Feidelson, Jr. (eds.), *The Modern Tradition*, pp. 551–52.

dwarf whose compensations are derisive laughter and constant truculence, his advice is quite useless. The cockfight perfectly illustrates the cruelty of natural competition, a competition in which the weak are always doomed. Abe Kusich identifies totally with the red cock. His passionate affection is the nearest thing to love we ever see in him, probably the nearest thing to love we see in any of the characters, and the cock's gallant fight seems to justify that love. Yet the cock's bravery is futile. The fight is unfair; the red cock is past his prime, and his beak is already cracked; his bravery, however extreme, is no match for Juju of the glossy feathers. Interestingly, the identification of Abe with the dead cock is matched by an identification of Earle and Miguel with the triumphant Juju. "They had combed their hair before leaving the garage, and their small round heads glistened prettily" (p. 129).

In that grotesque Darwinism which is the condition of life in *The Day of the Locust*, the rewards go only to the fittest—the rich and the handsome. Yet the modern victors are as debased and trivial as are modern gods and modern dreams. The "criminally handsome" Earle Shoop is a fool with "a two dimensional face" (p. 66), and the fortunate rich man is a "savage with pork-sausage fingers and a pimpled butt," "one of Mrs. Jenning's customers" (pp. 151–52). Faye's beauty is not only denied to Tod and Homer, but wasted on those to whom it is given, a waste almost like that in the marriage of Eula Varner to Flem Snopes.[29]

[29] Faulkner and West were friends in Hollywood, but, according to a letter from Faulkner to Cyril Schneider which Light cites, "they were friendly as hunters, not writers, and never talked of their own writing or the books of others." See Light, p. 146. There are, however, some

Tod's final bitterness toward Faye combines personal envy and impersonal anger. It is a condemnation of the waste and destruction in her destiny. And his impotence in the riot inspires, among other things, a moral terror. The self and all the standards by which it lives seem about to be obliterated in a spasm of violence, and the terror is intensified because the violence is understood. It has its unarguable logic. Apocalypse is an appropriate culmination of the themes first announced in *The Dream Life of Balso Snell*. *Balso* reveals the falseness of the world of dreams, art, and culture, and *Miss Lonelyhearts* presents the real victims of that falseness. In *The Day of the Locust*, the victims turn victimizers. The Burning of Los Angeles is the inevitable vengeance of those who, cheated by life, find that even their dreams have betrayed them.

---

obvious similarities in their work. For a discussion of the possible influence of *Sanctuary* on *The Day of the Locust*, see Carvel Collins, "Nathanael West's *The Day of the Locust* and *Sanctuary*."

Epilogue

Had he gone on there would have unfolded, I think, the
finest prose talent of our age.—William Carlos Williams.[1]

Williams' remark combines a rather pointless speculation
with a moving and generous tribute. Perhaps the tribute is
too generous. A talent like Faulkner's, for example, would
have been hard for West to surpass. And we cannot know
how West would have developed if he had not been killed.
He might have done things which would overshadow both
Miss Lonelyhearts and *The Day of the Locust,* and he might
never have written another novel. What he did do is small
but irreplaceable. It gives him a permanent importance beyond any might-have-been.

Yet there are more reasons for saluting Williams than for
quarreling with him. American writers, we are told, drift
inevitably into artistic disintegration and personal collapse,
but such a fate seems quite irrelevant to West. He obviously
matured as he got older. The excessive cleverness which
sometimes mars his early books yields to an increasing can-
dor. In *Balso Snell,* the only "confessional" moments—the

---

[1] William Carlos Williams, Review of *The Day of the Locust,* pp.
58–59.

John Gilson and Beagle Darwin sections—are surrounded
by such contortions of comic disguise that "serious" interpretation is impossible. *Miss Lonelyhearts* drops the protec-
tion of total ridicule and seriously examines some of West's
own preoccupations, but it embodies them in a character
from whom West remains distinct and toward whom his
attitude is still, in part, ironic. In *The Day of the Locust*,
protective irony entirely disappears. Tod's character is defined exactly, without deprecation or indulgence. He is a
witness whose authority and limitations are equally clear.

Confessional sincerity is not, of course, an adequate test
for a novel, especially that form of sincerity which merely
adds another footnote to the history of egoism. But in a
writer like West, disguise is a far more natural and therefore
dangerous tendency than exhibitionism. Even Miss Lonelyhearts reflects a double fantasy whose terms seem appropriate to West himself—the dream of being a savior, the fear
of being a fool. Given such preoccupations, mockery becomes ambiguously a threat to the self and a tempting alternative to its fears. It offers the illusion of immunity. The
mocker can deny both his inadequacies and his sufferings,
asserting a triumphant cleverness in their place. And for
West, the mocker's stance had an obvious fascination.
Throughout his first three novels, he alternately identifies
with it and rejects it, but is always obsessed by it. Shrike's
rhetoric is as persistent as a refrain. Beagle Darwin speaks it
in *Balso Snell* and Israel Satinpenny drops into a variation
of it in *A Cool Million*. In *The Day of the Locust*, however,
West briefly revives the same rhetoric for Claude Estee and
then drops it as if he were bored with it. It now seems tired,
as habitual and meaningless as the shop talk, gossip, and self-
conscious smut of Estee's guests. The party itself only de-

presses Tod. Its culminating expedition to Mrs. Jenning's whorehouse is both frivolous and dull, and its people are as ridiculous as Homer and Abe and Harry but not as interesting. They are dull because they are irrelevant. Tod instinctively turns away from them and seeks his clues in the bored masses and in those fringe performers who try to entertain them.

The Day of the Locust suggests, I think, that West had grown beyond the alternatives of mockery and pity. The world he confronts in it is repellent, but sensitive young men cannot save it and sardonic intellectuals cannot jeer it away. Roles which were inadequate are now simply irrelevant. They no longer interest West. What does interest him is the power latent in mass discontent, a power which will find its release quite independent of anyone's attempt to redeem it or laugh at it. The people who occupy West's attention now are, even in their deformities, more various and more subtly examined than the brilliant stereotypes of *Miss Lonelyhearts*. They cannot be reduced to the single quality of suffering. Nor, despite the truisms about West's distorted grotesques, can they be called Gothic or synthetically perverse. Their counterparts are depressingly common, visible in any bus station, and West quietly recognizes both his own kinship with them and his alienation from them. The problem itself now absorbs his interest, not the question of appropriate stances toward it.

West's style establishes the cool precision of his portraits. Despite his love of masks, his prose is both unmannered and unadorned, so bare that any lapse will show. There is no adverbial padding in his sentences, no swell of rhetoric, no self-conscious terseness or muscular lyricism. The idiom is, in Williams' phrase,[2] "plain American," but it absorbs without strain anything from parody to abstract comment. And, unlike many of our literary fashions, West's style emphasizes lucid interpretation. He always reduces incoherence to summary paraphrase. The chaotic speeches of Doyle and Homer are, for example, interpreted, not recorded. The reveries of his characters are equally succinct, expressed in images which are both psychologically and thematically appropriate. Violent action in his novels always carries a clear sense of its motives and its consequences; it is always gesture, not just melodrama. Obviously, as I have already remarked, clarity has its limitations as well as its virtues. West was not the complete literary artist or the definitive stylist of our time. He was, however, a distinctive and intelligent analyst of materials which are everywhere in modern literature and modern life.

West's recurrent themes—actor-audience, order-disorder, deadness-violence, dream-misery—are finally reducible to terms so banal they are probably profound. Inarticulate desire supplies the eruptive force in each of these themes, a force so common in life that it is reflected in clichés as wearily familiar as "I can't express it." And even in literature it is hardly the special property of Anderson and West. Faulkner's Benjy, Steinbeck's Lennie, and O'Neill's Hairy Ape are only a few of the more obvious variants upon a familiar type. And the masses, especially in the thirties, have commanded nearly as much literary attention as individual primitives. The theme of decadent exhaustion is equally familiar. It is everywhere in the symbolists, the *fin de siècle*

[2] Williams, "Sordid? Good God!" p. 5.

writers, and the early poetry of T. S. Eliot. It is also reflected in the attempt to revitalize—even rebarbarize—language, an attempt which has obsessed many of the century's best writers. Lawrence's urge to discover a pure sensual communication, to destroy consciousness and all the traditional gods which inhabit it, derived, of course, from his conviction that our gods had died, that our language—the things by which we define and express ourselves—had worn out. Hemingway's famous repudiation of abstract words is perhaps another example.[3] And we need only recall Joyce's experiments in language—or the ubiquity of ironic parallels in which the banality of the present is compared to a myth of the past—to realize how common the theme of decadence and exhaustion has been. In many ways, primitive seeking and mass suffering and decadent collapse are all aspects of a single theme. "I can't express it" could almost be called *the* modern problem. Or, if an assertion so broad seems fatuous, I shall merely point out that modern fiction has long been obsessed with the submerged—with those individuals who are submerged in society and those impulses which are submerged in consciousness, with all that is buried, thwarted, denied expression, all that cannot speak.

More than a metaphor connects these various forms of thwarting. Coherent expression is, of course, the crucial test of any personality or any culture. Its alternatives are deadness and disorder, sterile forms and destructive violence. West's anatomy of collapse is as relevant to the politics of

[3] "There were many words that you could not stand to hear and finally only the names of places had dignity. . . . Abstract words such as glory, honor, courage, or hallow were obscene beside the concrete names of villages, the numbers of roads, the names of rivers, the numbers of regiments and the dates." Hemingway, *A Farewell to Arms* (New York: Bantam Books, 1954), p. 137.

the self as it is to the politics of any state. Perhaps more clearly than any writer we have had, West understood the connection between neurotic aesthetes and vulgar masses, between the dreams of art and the stereotypes of popular culture, between the violence of a mob and the violence in himself. And he revealed the implications of decadence with equal clarity. Parody was, for him, a diagnostic instrument. He used it to identify the familiar themes of our culture, expose their characteristic weaknesses, and express the fact of their decadence. When "classic" ideas or actions collapse into banalities, parody becomes a disturbingly adequate description of them. They are dead, they have no capacity for further change, and the implications of their fates assume syllogistic certainty. In West's novels, decadence is nearly absolute. The violence and suffering he portrays are the inevitable accompaniments of collapse. Though life is not all like that, some life is always like that and all life is in perpetual danger of becoming like that. His "prophetic" vision need not come true at any particular time. It defines the failure which always awaits us, the possibility against which all affirmative action contends.

Selected Bibliography

For additional listings, consult the bibliographies compiled by William White, which are listed under "Critical and Biographical Studies" below.

Works of Nathanael West

(In Order of Publication)

The Dream Life of Balso Snell. Paris and New York: Contact Editions, 1931.
Miss Lonelyhearts. New York: Liveright, 1933.
A Cool Million. New York: Covici-Friede, 1934.
The Day of the Locust. New York: Random House, 1939.
"Some Notes on Violence," *Contact,* I (October, 1932), 132–33.
"Christmass Poem," *Contempo,* III (February 21, 1933), 6.
"Some Notes on Miss Lonelyhearts," *Contempo,* III (May 15, 1933), 1–2.
"Business Deal," *Americana,* I (October, 1933), 14–15.
"Soft Soap for the Barber," *New Republic,* LXXXI (November, 1934), 23.

American Reprints

The Dream Life of Balso Snell and A Cool Million. New York: Noonday Press, 1963.
The Dream Life of Balso Snell and A Cool Million. New York: Avon, 1965.
Miss Lonelyhearts. New York: New Directions, n.d.

Miss Lonelyhearts. New York: Avon, 1964.
Miss Lonelyhearts and The Day of the Locust. Norfolk, Conn.: New Directions Paperbooks, 1962.
The Day of the Locust. New York: New Directions, 1950.
The Day of the Locust. New York: Bantam Books, 1962.
The Complete Works of Nathanael West. New York: Farrar, Straus and Cudahy, 1957.

Critical and Biographical Studies

Aaron, Daniel. "Late Thoughts on Nathanael West," *Massachusetts Review,* VI (Winter–Spring, 1965), 307–17.
————. "The Truly Monstrous: A Note on Nathanael West," *Partisan Review,* XIV (February, 1947), 98–106.
————. "Waiting for the Apocalypse," *Hudson Review,* III (Winter, 1951), 634–36.
Andreach, Robert. "Nathanael West's *Miss Lonelyhearts:* Between the Dead Pan and the Unborn Christ," *Modern Fiction Studies,* XIII (Summer, 1966), 251–60.
Collins, Carvel. "Nathanael West's *The Day of the Locust* and *Sanctuary,*" *Faulkner Studies,* II (Summer, 1953), 23–24.
Comerchero, Victor. *Nathanael West: The Ironic Prophet.* Syracuse: Syracuse University Press, 1964.
Cowley, Malcolm. "It's the Telling That Counts," *New York Times Book Review* (May 12, 1957), 4–5.
Daniel, Carter A. "West's Revisions of *Miss Lonelyhearts,*" *Studies in Bibliography,* XVI (1963), 232–43.
Flores, Angel. "Miss Lonelyhearts in the Haunted Castle," *Contempo,* III (July 25, 1933), 1.
Galloway, David D. "Nathanael West's Dream Dump," *Critique,* VI (Winter, 1963–1964), 46–64.
————. "A Picaresque Apprenticeship: Nathanael West's *The Dream Life of Balso Snell* and *A Cool Million,*" *Wisconsin Studies in Contemporary Literature,* V (Summer, 1964), 110–26.
Herbst, Josephine. "Hunter of Doves," *Botteghe Oscure,* XIII (1954), 310–44.
————. "Nathanael West," *Kenyon Review,* XXIII (Autumn, 1961), 611–30.
Houston, James D. "Three Varieties of Grotesquerie in Twentieth Century American Fiction." Unpublished Master's thesis, Department of English, Stanford University, 1962.

Hyman, Stanley Edgar. *Nathanael West*. University of Minnesota Pamphlets on American Writers. Minneapolis: University of Minnesota Press, 1962.

Liebling, A. J. "Shed a Tear for Mr. West," *New York World Telegram*, June 24, 1933, p. 14.

Light, James F. "Miss Lonelyhearts: The Imagery of Nightmare," *American Quarterly*, VIII (Winter, 1956), 316–27.

————. *Nathanael West: An Interpretative Study*. Evanston: Northwestern University Press, 1961.

————. "Nathanael West and the Ravaging Locust," *American Quarterly*, XII (Spring, 1960), 44–54.

————. "Violence, Dreams, and Dostoevsky: The Art of Nathanael West," *College English*, XIX (February, 1958), 208–13.

Lokke, V. L. "A Side Glance at Medusa: Hollywood, the Literature Boys, and Nathanael West," *Southwest Review*, XLVI (Winter, 1961), 35–45.

Lorch, Thomas M. "West's *Miss Lonelyhearts*: Skepticism Mitigated?" *Renascence*, XVIII (Winter, 1966), 90–109.

Peden, William. "Nathanael West," *Virginia Quarterly Review*, XXXIII (Summer, 1957), 468–72.

Perelman, S. J. "Nathanael West: A Portrait," *Contempo*, III (July 25, 1933), 4.

Podhoretz, Norman. "A Particular Kind of Joking," *New Yorker*, May 18, 1957, pp. 156–65.

Ratner, Marc L. " 'Anywhere Out of This World : Baudelaire and Nathanael West," *American Literature*, XXXI (January, 1960), 456–63.

Rosenfeld, Isaac. "Faulkner and Contemporaries," *Partisan Review*, XVIII (January–February, 1951), 106–14.

Sanford, John. "Nathanael West," *The Screen Writer*, II (December, 1946), 10–13.

Schneider, Cyril M. "The Individuality of Nathanael West," *Western Review*, XX (Autumn, 1955), 7–28.

Tibbetts, A. M. "The Strange Half-World of Nathanael West," *Prairie Schooner*, XXXIV (Spring, 1960), 8–14.

Volpe, Edmond L. "The Waste Land of Nathanael West," *Renascence*, XIII (Winter, 1961), 69–77.

White, William. "Nathanael West: A Bibliography," *Studies in Bibliography*, XI (1958), 207–24.

————. "Bibliography of Nathanael West," *Book Collector*, II (Autumn, 1962), 351.

———. "Nathanael West: A Bibliography Addenda," *Serif,* II (March, 1965), 5–18.

Williams, William Carlos, Review of *The Day of the Locust, Tomorrow,* X (November, 1950), 58–59.

———. "Sordid? Good God!" *Contempo,* III (July 25, 1933), 5.

Wilson, Edmund. "Postscript," *The Boys in the Back Room.* San Francisco: The Colt Press, 1951.

Sources and Background

Aaron, Daniel. *Writers on the Left: Episodes in American Literary Communism.* New York: Harcourt, Brace & World, Inc., 1961.

Anderson, Sherwood. *Winesburg, Ohio.* New York: Penguin Books, 1946.

Baudelaire, Charles. *The Flowers of Evil: A Selection.* Edited by Marthiel and Jackson Mathews. New York: New Directions Paperbooks, 1955.

———. *Prose and Poetry.* Translated by Arthur Symons. New York: Albert and Charles Boni, 1926.

Breton, André. *Le surréalisme et la peinture.* Paris: Librairie Gallimard, 1928.

Bunyan, John. *Grace Abounding to the Chief of Sinners.* Oxford: Oxford University Press, 1962.

———. *The Pilgrim's Progress.* London: J. M. Dent and Co., 1898.

Cabell, James Branch. *Jurgen.* London: The Bodley Head Limited, 1921.

Ellmann, Richard, and Charles Feidelson, Jr. (eds.). *The Modern Tradition: Backgrounds of Modern Literature.* New York: Oxford University Press, 1965.

Fowlie, Wallace. *Age of Surrealism.* The Swallow Press and William Morrow and Co., Inc., 1950.

———. *Clowns and Angels: Studies in Modern French Literature.* New York: Sheed & Ward, 1943.

Grosz, George. "Self Portrait of the Artist," *Americana,* I (November, 1932), 22.

Haesaerts, Paul, and James Ensor. *Ensor.* New York: Harry N. Abrams, Inc., 1959.

Hellman, Lillian. "The Art of the Theater I," *Paris Review,* No. 33 (Winter–Spring, 1965), 65–95.

Herzberg, Max J. (ed.) *The Reader's Encyclopedia of American Literature.* New York: Thomas Y. Crowell Company, 1962.

Howe, Irving. *Sherwood Anderson.* "The American Men of Letters Series." William Sloane Associates, 1951.

Huxley, Aldous. *Antic Hay and The Giaconda Smile.* New York: Harper and Brothers, 1951.

Huysmans, Joris-Karl. *Against the Grain.* New York: Modern Library, 1930.

————. *Down Stream and Other Works.* Translated by Samuel Putnam. Chicago: Pascal Covici, 1927.

————. *En Route.* Translated by C. Kegan Paul. London: Kegan Paul, Trench, Trubner & Co., Ltd., 1918.

————. *Là Bas.* Translated by Keene Wallis. Chicago: The Black Archer Press, 1935

James, William. *The Varieties of Religious Experience.* New York: Modern Library, n.d.

Machen, Arthur. *The Hill of Dreams.* New York: Alfred A. Knopf, 1924.

Motherwell, Robert (ed.). *The Dada Painters and Poets: An Anthology.* New York: Wittenborn, Shultz, Inc., 1951.

Nadeau, Maurice. *Histoire du Surréalisme.* Paris: Editions du Seuil, 1945.

Perelman, S. J. "The Art of Fiction," *Paris Review,* No. 30 (1963), 147–64.

————. *The Most of S. J. Perelman.* New York: Simon & Schuster, 1958.

Pia, Pascal. *Baudelaire.* Translated by Patrick Gregory. New York: Grove Press, 1961.

Rimbaud, Arthur. *Illuminations and Other Prose Poems.* Translated by Louise Varèse. New York: New Directions Paperbooks, 1957.

————. *A Season in Hell and The Drunken Boat.* Translated by Louise Varèse. Norfolk, Conn.: New Directions Paperbooks, 1961.

Seldes, Gilbert. *The Seven Lively Arts.* New York: Harper and Brothers, 1924.

Ward, Lynd. *God's Man: A Novel in Woodcuts.* New York: Jonathan Cape & Harrison Smith, Inc., 1930.

————. *Madman's Drum: A Novel in Woodcuts.* New York: Jonathan Cape & Harrison Smith, Inc., 1930.

Waugh, Coulton, *The Comics.* New York: The Macmillan Company, 1947.

Wilson, Edmund. *Axel's Castle: A Study in the Imaginative Literature of 1870–1930.* New York: Charles Scribner's Sons, 1947.

Index